COMPREHENSIVE RESEARCH
AND STUDY GUIDE

BLOOM'S
MAJOR
DRAMATISTS

Henrik
Ibsen

EDITED AND WITH AN
INTRODUCTION BY HAROLD BLOOM

CURRENTLY AVAILABLE

BLOOM'S MAJOR DRAMATISTS

Anton Chekhov

Henrik Ibsen

Arthur Miller

Eugene O'Neill

Shakespeare's Comedies

Shakespeare'sHistories

Shakespeare's Romances

Shakespeare's Tragedies

George Bernard Shaw

Tennessee Williams

BLOOM'S MAJOR NOVELISTS

Jane Austen

The Brontës

Willa Cather

Charles Dickens

William Faulkner

F. Scott Fitzgerald

Nathaniel Hawthorne

Ernest Hemingway

Toni Morrison

John Steinbeck

Mark Twain

Alice Walker

BLOOM'S MAJOR SHORT STORY WRITERS

William Faulkner

F. Scott Fitzgerald

Ernest Hemingway

O. Henry

James Joyce

Herman Melville

Flannery O'Connor

Edgar Allan Poe

J. D. Salinger

John Steinbeck

Mark Twain

Eudora Welty

BLOOM'S MAJOR WORLD POETS

Geoffrey Chaucer

Emily Dickinson

John Donne

T. S. Eliot

Robert Frost

Langston Hughes

John Milton

Edgar Allan Poe

Shakespeare's Poems & Sonnets

Alfred, Lord Tennyson

Walt Whitman

William Wordsworth

BLOOM'S NOTES

The Adventures of Huckleberry Finn

Aeneid

The Age of Innocence

Animal Farm

The Autobiography of Malcolm X

The Awakening

Beloved

Beowulf

Billy Budd, Benito Cereno, & Bartleby the Scrivener

Brave New World

The Catcher in the Rye

Crime and Punishment

The Crucible

Death of a Salesman

A Farewell to Arms

Frankenstein

The Grapes of Wrath

Great Expectations

The Great Gatsby

Gulliver's Travels

Hamlet

Heart of Darkness & The Secret Sharer

Henry IV, Part One

I Know Why the Caged Bird Sings

Iliad

Inferno

Invisible Man

Jane Eyre

Julius Caesar

King Lear

Lord of the Flies

Macbeth

A Midsummer Night's Dream

Moby-Dick

Native Son

Nineteen Eighty-Four

Odyssey

Oedipus Plays

Of Mice and Men

The Old Man and the Sea

Othello

Paradise Lost

The Portrait of a Lady

A Portrait of the Artist as a Young Man

Pride and Prejudice

The Red Badge of Courage

Romeo and Juliet

The Scarlet Letter

Silas Marner

The Sound and the Fury

The Sun Also Rises

A Tale of Two Cities

Tess of the D'Urbervilles

Their Eyes Were Watching God

To Kill a Mockingbird

Uncle Tom's Cabin

Wuthering Heights

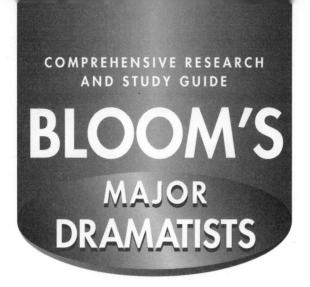

COMPREHENSIVE RESEARCH
AND STUDY GUIDE

BLOOM'S

MAJOR
DRAMATISTS

Henrik
Ibsen

EDITED AND WITH AN INTRODUCTION
BY HAROLD BLOOM

First Printing
1 3 5 7 9 8 6 4 2

Library of Congress Cataloging-in-Publication Data

Henrik Ibsen / edited and with an introduction by Harold Bloom.
p.   cm.—(Bloom's major dramatists)
Includes bibliographical references and index.
ISBN 0-7910-5239-7
1. Ibsen, Henrik, 1828–1906—Examinations—Study guides.
I. Bloom, Harold.   II. Series.
PT8895.H43   1999b
839.8'226—dc21
99-15682
CIP

Chelsea House Publishers
1974 Sproul Road, Suite 400
Broomall, PA 19008-0914

The Chelsea House World Wide Website address is
http://www.chelseahouse.com

Contributing Editor: Erica Da Costa

Contents

User's Guide

This volume is designed to present biographical, critical, and bibliographical information on the playwright's best-known or most important works. Following Harold Bloom's editor's note and introduction are a detailed biography of the author, discussing major life events and important literary accomplishments. A plot summary of each play follows, tracing significant themes, patterns, and motifs in the work.

A selection of critical extracts, derived from previously published material from leading critics, analyzes aspects of each play. The extracts consist of statements from the author, if available, early reviews of the work, and later evaluations up to the present. A bibliography of the author's writings (including a complete list of all works written, cowritten, edited, and translated), a list of additional books and articles on the author and his or her work, and an index of themes and ideas in the author's writings conclude the volume.

～

Harold Bloom is Sterling Professor of the Humanities at Yale University and Henry W. and Albert A. Berg Professor of English at the New York University Graduate School. He is the author of over 20 books and the editor of more than 30 anthologies of literary criticism.

Professor Bloom's works include *Shelley's Mythmaking* (1959), *The Visionary Company* (1961), *Blake's Apocalypse* (1963), *Yeats* (1970), *A Map of Misreading* (1975), *Kabbalah and Criticism* (1975), and *Agon: Toward a Theory of Revisionism* (1982). *The Anxiety of Influence* (1973) sets forth Professor Bloom's provocative theory of the literary relationships between the great writers and their predecessors. His most recent books include *The American Religion* (1992), *The Western Canon* (1994), *Omens of Millennium: The Gnosis of Angels, Dreams, and Resurrection* (1996), and *Shakespeare: The Invention of the Human* (1998), a finalist for the 1998 National Book Award.

Professor Bloom earned his Ph.D. from Yale University in 1955 and has served on the Yale faculty since then. He is a 1985 MacArthur Foundation Award recipient, served as the Charles Eliot Norton Professor of Poetry at Harvard University in 1987–88, and has received honorary degrees from the universities of Rome and Bologna. In 1999, Professor Bloom received the prestigious American Academy of Arts and Letters Gold Medal for Criticism.

Currently, Harold Bloom is the editor of numerous Chelsea House volumes of literary criticism, including the series BLOOM'S NOTES, BLOOM'S MAJOR SHORT STORY WRITERS, BLOOM'S MAJOR POETS, MAJOR LITERARY CHARACTERS, MODERN CRITICAL VIEWS, MODERN CRITICAL INTERPRETATIONS, and WOMEN WRITERS OF ENGLISH AND THEIR WORKS.

Editor's Note

The major Ibsen critics represented here includes George Bernard Shaw, Eric Bentley, Rolf Fjelde, Michael Meyer, Inga-Stina Ewbank, and John Northam. Besides Shaw, authors and notables commenting upon Ibsen are E. M. Forster, Arthur Miller, Leo Lowenthal, and George Groddeck. The range of interest in Ibsen is no longer as comprehensive as it once was, but one can prophesy that Ibsen always returns, since no dramatist since—not even Pirandello or Beckett—has achieved his eminence.

Introduction

HAROLD BLOOM

My favorite plays by Ibsen would include *Brand* and the epic *Emperor and Galilean*, as well as *Peer Gynt* and *Heda Gabbler*. Only the latter two are considered in this little volume, together with the late visionary dramas, *The Master Builder* and *When We Dead Awaken*.

I regret that the revised edition of Brian Johnston's *The Ibsen Cycle* (1992) came into my hands too late for me to excerpt from it either in my *Henrik Ibsen: Modern Critical Views* (1999) or this brief book. Though previously I had been baffled by Johnston's insistence on the close parallel between Hegel's *Phenomenology of Mind* and Ibsen's final twelve plays, Johnston indeed does demonstrate that Ibsen's work fits very well into the Hegelian vision of tragedy. Whether or not this resulted from the direct influences upon Ibsen, like Shakespeare and Hegel, Ibsen is a world-visionary who works on a vast scale. Parallels between the three necessarily abound.

Brand and the Emperor Julian are Ibsen's most heroic characters, yet they are hero-villains in the Shakespearean mode. This doubleness applies still more strongly to Hedda Gabler, and to later figures like Solness and Rubek. For Thomas Van Laan, Hedda Gabler is a version of Shakespeare's Cleopatra; I would add Iago to the mix. The Ibsenite hero-villains, like the Shakespearean, are trollish or daemonic; the great exception is Peer Gynt, whose comic genius (like Falstaff's), redeems him from most taints of trollishness. The Emperor Julian has his Macbeth-aspect, but Peer is natural man, an amiable scamp who may behave like a hero-villain, but who charms himself, his fellow-characters, and the audience into forgiving everything. Call Peer Gynt, like Ibsen himself, a borderline troll, but far gentler than his fiercer creator. For Ibsen's true self-portrait, we can turn to Hedda Gabbler, a worthy rival of Shakespeare's Cleopatra. ❀

Biography of
Henrik Ibsen

Henrik Ibsen was born in Skien, Norway, a coastal town of about 3,000 inhabitants, on March 20, 1828. Norway, at the time, was an underdeveloped country with virtually no culture of its own. Denmark had ruled Norway for more than 400 years until 1814 when it gained independence. Almost immediately, however, Norway came under Swedish rule, but Sweden would exert little power over the Norwegians. Culturally, Norwegians remained under the influence of Denmark: Norwegians read Danish literature, Danish translations of English and French literature, and the written Norwegian language, *riksmaal*, was almost indistinguishable from written Danish. The tension between Danish and Norwegian cultures was to figure largely into Ibsen's early life and work.

In Ibsen's young adulthood, Norwegians began an earnest search for their own identity, their own traditions and national origins. Of the little existing Norwegian literature the Icelandic Sagas, written six centuries earlier by Norwegian adventurers who reached Iceland, would particularly fascinate and inspire Ibsen.

For Ibsen's first seven years, his parents were prosperous and social people. This changed completely, however, as financial ruin took hold of them. By 1836, Ibsen's father had been forced to mortgage or sell most of his possessions. The family never recovered in any sense, but Ibsen's father especially would never regain any peace or happiness. At the age of 15 Ibsen was apprenticed to an apothecary in Grimstad, a tiny community 100 miles south of Skien. There he lived meagerly in cramped quarters with the apothecary, his family, and his servants. In 1846 he fathered an illegitimate son, born to him by one of the servant girls. Though he would fulfill his financial obligation to the child, Ibsen would never know this son. It was here in Grimstad that he wrote his first play, *Catiline*.

In pursuit of a medical degree, Ibsen moved to Christiania (now Oslo) and began studying to enter the university in 1850, but he was ultimately unable to pass his matriculation examinations. By the time he failed his entrance exams, however, he was more interested in theater than medicine, *Catiline* having been published, and his second play, *The Warrior's Barrow*, having been produced at the Christiania Theater. His first two plays secured for him an appointment as "theater-poet" of the brand-new Bergen National Theater. The founders of this theater wanted specifically to develop a Norwegian national theater, as free of the Danish influence as possible. This would prove to be an impossible goal. It was here that Ibsen wrote five unremarkable plays, all in verse form. In Bergen, he also met his wife, Suzannah Thorensen, whom he would marry in 1858. They would have a complicated, somewhat contentious marriage, but ultimately successful and happy. They would produce one child, Sigurd, who was born in 1859.

In 1857, Ibsen left the Bergen Theater and became director of the Norwegian Theater of Christiania. This also was a new institution, established by those extreme patriots who were angry about the Bergen Theater's failure to continue its original mission. The Christiania Theater went bankrupt, however, and its closure helped spur Ibsen's decision in 1864 to leave Norway for what became a 27-year voluntary exile. He had, by this time, become highly suspect of the very idea of a Norwegian national theater, and even more so of his compatriots, who had received his plays very badly. He increasingly perceived Norwegians as unenlightened. He would live primarily in Italy and Germany during the following years, but would never remain for long in any one town—Rome, Arriccia, Frascati, Ishia, Sorrento, Amalfi, Berchtesgarden, Kitzbuhel, Dresden, Gossensass, Munich. Yet he obsessed about Norway, writing about it, setting his plays there, and making frequent proclamations that he would never return to the petty, small-mindedness that pervaded the country.

In Italy, he wrote the volcanic *Brand* (1866), which finally made a reputation for him and won him a stipend from the Norwegian government. It also established him in Scandinavia as the leader of the revolt against dead thought and tradition. He would attack political conservatism and liberalism, insincere religiosity, and bourgeois values. He would often depict characters who were emotionally bankrupt, leading many to believe that he himself was emotionally deficient; to some degree, they were right.

He was an advocate of youth and those who were willing to "commit a madness." (Upon seeing Michaelangelo's work for the first time, Ibsen immediately determined that the sculptor had committed a madness.) His plays describe a struggle against the dark forces within one's own soul, which Ibsen felt was one of life's overarching themes—the fight with the inner troll. With *Pillars of Society* in 1877, he became an international figure and the foremost dramatist of his age. His plays, however successful they were with audiences, never met with unanimous admiration. He was reviled and defamed throughout his life for his bold ideas and scandalous characters.

He reinvented theater by insisting on a naturalness of acting and using modern colloquial dialogue. He dispensed with the old artifices of theater such as monologues, comical asides to the audience, mistaken identities, and overheard conversations. He also created a "double-density" dialogue for his characters in which they would say one thing but mean something else. This was a kind of subtlety that had never been put on the stage before.

In 1889, Ibsen began an affair with a much younger women named Emilie Bardach. This would be the first of four such affairs, all with very young women. He seemed to draw a good deal of strength and inspiration from these women, and they turned up, sometimes conspicuously, in his plays. Ibsen became preoccupied with the idea of youth as he grew older. He feared it, admired it, and required it.

Near the end of his life he would return to Norway, wanting badly to be near the sea. In 1900, Ibsen suffered the first of several incapacitating strokes. He died in Oslo on May 23, 1906. In a tribute to Ibsen, the poet Rainier Maria Rilke addressed him after his death: "Loneliest of men, withdrawn from all, how rapidly have they overtaken you by means of your fame! But lately they were fundamentally opposed to you, and now they treat you as their equal. And they carry your words about with them in cages of their presumption, and exhibit them in the streets and excite them a little from their own safe distance: all those wild beasts of yours." ❀

Plot Summary of
Hedda Gabler

George Tesman, having just arrived home from his honeymoon abroad with his new wife, Hedda, is looking forward to a professorial appointment at the university which his friend, Judge Brack, has assured him will be secured soon. Miss Juliana Tesman, George's old aunt, is present to greet them. She lavishes maternal attention on her nephew, who himself is devoted to her for raising him after his parents died. They are a mutual admiration society. They are well-meaning but complacent and unimaginative people, and this clearly drives Hedda to distraction. George Tesman drops hints that Hedda is pregnant, but Hedda constantly bristles at any talk of it—this is not a pregnancy she wanted.

Mrs. Thea Elvsted, a figure from both Hedda's and George's pasts, calls on them. Hedda had gone to school with Thea, and George had once courted her. Thea confides secretly to Hedda that she has run away from a loveless marriage and that she has followed Eilert Løvborg into town. Eilert was living in the Elvsted household as teacher to Mr. Elvsted's children, but he published a successful book and abandoned his position to look for something more auspicious. Thea and Eilert became very close in the Elvsted house. She had been his secretary and his muse while he worked on the book. She feels she must be near him. She begs the Tesmans to make Eilert feel welcome, since he has, as is suggested, a number of enemies.

Eilert had been a literary rival to George and was once Hedda's lover. Eilert is the passionate man whom Hedda should have married, but his shady past made it a social impossibility. His sudden reentrance throws her off-balance.

Judge Brack informs George that Eilert's appearance has cast doubt on the university position on which George had been counting. George panics because he has recently purchased a house he could not afford, which he believes is the house Hedda had always wanted. Though worried about his own finances, Tesman is not a vindictive man and invites Eilert to a party with Judge Brack and himself. Eilert greets Hedda as "Hedda Gabler" letting her know that he does not respect her marriage, but she refuses to engage him further, admitting her terrible fear of scandal.

At the party Eilert reads part of the manuscript of his new book to George Tesman, who finds it excellent. They become somewhat drunk and on his way home from the party, Eilert drops his manuscript on the ground. George finds it and rescues it. He shows it to Hedda, telling her what a masterpiece it is. When Eilert, completely distraught, shows up at the Tesman's to tell them that he has lost his manuscript, he is met by Hedda alone who feigns ignorance of the whole affair. He feels he is ruined by the loss of it and tells her he is leaving, so Hedda gives him one of her pistols—a pistol that was her father's and which she is fond of shooting. Hedda indirectly encourages him to use it on himself. He leaves and Hedda burns the manuscript in a fire.

Eilert does indeed kill himself after telling Thea Elvsted that he had ripped the manuscript into a million shreds, this manuscript she had so faithfully helped him transcribe. He cannot bear to tell her that he lost it. Thea goes to the Tesmans and declares that she has thousands of scraps and notes from the writing of the book. George Tesman decides to devote himself to putting the manuscript back together from Thea's notes.

Judge Brack gives Hedda a report of Eilert's death scene, which turns out to be an ill-executed suicide in the house of a prostitute. Hedda had hoped for something much more "beautiful." Brack also tells her about a potential scandal beginning to simmer around the fact that the pistol Eilert used belonged to Hedda. She knows she cannot weather a scandal, and so she kills herself with another of her father's pistols.

In analyzing this work we see that Hedda longs to be like Eilert Løvborg but is too much of a coward. Eilert represents the liberated spirit, outside of society, full of the life impulse Hedda lacks. Hedda's bleak, emotional life and her submission to her darker impulses are not a product of society but of her own "trollish" nature. The troll is a figure from Norwegian folklore, a playful yet demonic imp, which Ibsen used repeatedly throughout his plays to symbolize a darkness within one's own soul. Trollishness has been described as something "destructive of most human values, yet it seems the inevitable shadow side of energies and talents that exceed the human measure" (Harold Bloom, *The Western Canon*). Though

Ibsen does not specifically refer to the "inner-troll" in *Hedda Gabler*, it is perhaps because Hedda is the complete expression of troll, full of a vitality and curiosity that has gone past mischievousness and turned sour.

Ibsen often wrote about societal ills and injustices but never without creating fully realized characters and specific struggles to depict them. In *Hedda Gabler,* however, Ibsen is expressly not criticizing the pervading social order. Ibsen tried to make this quite clear when he said, "I have not tried in this play to deal with so-called problems. My main object was to portray human beings, human moods, and human destinies, as conditioned by certain relevant social conditions and attitudes."

Hedda's fiendish nature is emboldened by the fact that she lacks any clear direction for her life. She has given away what freedom she had to marry a man she does not love and become pregnant with a child she does not want. Hedda's father's pistols symbolize her repressed self, and her propensity for firing them into the air is a picture of the aimlessness of her existence.

George Tesman is wholly antagonistic to Hedda though he is a good man. He, along with his old aunt and lifelong maid Berta, is dull and conventional. These three are not striving for self-realization as Hedda is, because they suit themselves perfectly just as they are. Ibsen clarified the point himself: "Tesman, his old aunts and the faithful servant Berta together form a picture of complete unity. They think alike, they share the same memories, and have the same outlook on life. To Hedda they appear like a strange and hostile power, aimed at her very being. In a performance of the play, the harmony that exists between them must be conveyed." Yet, we must remember what Hedda herself declared to be her dominant emotion—the fear of scandal. A recurring phrase in *Hedda Gabler,* uttered by both Hedda and George is, "Nobody behaves that way around here." In this, she is quintessential bourgeois and hates herself for it.

Herman Bang, a Danish admirer of Ibsen's, said, "Most of Ibsen's plays had been about egotistical men and selfless women; but here was a play about an egotistical woman, and whereas a man's egotism may at least often cause him to accomplish much, a woman's merely drives her into isolation and self-adoration. Hedda has no source of richness in herself and must constantly seek it in others so that her life becomes a pursuit of sensation and experiment; and her hatred of bearing a child is the ultimate expression of her egotism, the sickness that brings death."

Herman Bang was certainly not typical of Ibsen's audiences. In general, *Hedda Gabler* baffled contemporary audiences partly because Ibsen refused to use explanatory monologues, long speeches that would be unnatural for a "real" person to make, and over-extended dialogue, which was used for purposes of exposition. Ibsen let the story unfold through the characters' actions and inter-actions, though the conventions of the time were far more oriented toward spectacle and grand theatricality. The presentation of a truer reality was disturbing and at times incomprehensible to Ibsen's audience, though now it has become absolutely traditional.

Another of Ibsen's contributions to theater was a kind a multi-layered dialogue in which characters spoke obliquely about a subject rather than directly. In the following exchange between Hedda and Judge Brack, the subject is Hedda's unfulfilling marriage. Brack also makes the scandalous proposal that Hedda engage with him in an affair.

> BRACK: All I want is to have a warm circle of intimate friends, where I can be of use one way or another, with the freedom to come and go as—as a trusted friend—
>
> HEDDA: Of the man of the house, you mean?
>
> BRACK: (with a bow) Frankly—I prefer the lady. But the man, too, of course, in his place. That kind of—let's say triangular arrange-ment—you can't imagine how satisfying it can be all around.
>
> HEDDA: Yes, I must say I longed for some third person so many times on that trip. Oh—those endless tête-à-têtes in railway compartments! —
>
> BRACK: Fortunately the wedding trip's over now.
>
> HEDDA: The trip will go on—and on. I've only come to one stop on the line.
>
> BRACK: Well, then what you do is jump out—and stretch yourself a little, Mrs. Hedda.
>
> HEDDA: I'll never jump out.

As obvious as the interchange may be to the modern reader, Ibsen was accused of being obscure.

In this scene, Brack tries to blackmail Hedda sexually since her husband is financially beholden to him. Brack also knows she will have little opportunity for excitement in her life as a professor's wife. Hedda is bored, but not bored enough to implicate herself in a possible public embarrassment. By the end of the play she is also presumably at Brack's mercy for his part in the suppression of the oncoming scandal. With this realization, her fate is inevitable. When she does finally turn her gun on herself, George, true to form shrieks, "People don't do such things!" He is shocked as much by the outrageousness and impropriety of the action, as by the result—the death of Hedda Gabler. ❀

List of Characters in
Hedda Gabler

Hedda Gabler is married to George Tesman, but she is not in love with her husband, an amiable but self-satisfied academic. In fact, Hedda finds her bourgeois life with George suffocating. When Hedda's ex-lover, Eilert Løvborg, is reintroduced into her life, Hedda decides to destroy him and his vitality, which remind her of her own desires, now buried for the sake of a respectable marriage.

George Tesman is a well-meaning professor whose specialty is domestic handicrafts of the Middle Ages. He has married the unpredictable daughter of General Gabler, Hedda.

Miss Juliana Tesman is George's old aunt, who hovers around him like a guardian angel. She, along with another old aunt, raised George after his parents died, and she is extremely proud of him. She is happy about his union with Hedda and determines to continue looking after both of them.

A former classmate of Hedda's, **Thea Elvsted** has run away from a loveless marriage. She confides in Hedda that she has come to town in pursuit of Eilert Løvborg, to whom she is completely devoted.

Judge Brack is an important local figure and good friend to George Tesman. He has helped George purchase the new house they are in, and he secures a post for George at the university. His designs are not entirely benign, however, since he desires Hedda.

Hedda's ex-lover and former friend of George, **Eilert Løvborg** has recently reappeared in town on the strength of the success of a new book he has written. Løvborg has had a difficult past, as everyone surreptitiously alludes to. He disappeared entirely several years previous and was reformed while working honestly as a tutor to Mr. Elvsted's children. There he met Thea Elvsted, and together they worked on the book that has made him a recent success as well as a new book that has not yet been published.

Berta is the maid who has recently come to serve at the new Tesman household, having come from George's former home with his aunts. Juliana Tesman, George Tesman, and Berta form a triangle of contented domesticity and happiness, which Hedda finds threatening. ❀

Critical Views on
Hedda Gabler

GEORGE BERNARD SHAW ON HEDDA'S DESIRES

[George Bernard Shaw (1856–1950) is best known as the author of such plays as *Pygmalion, Heartbreak House,* and *Three Plays for Puritans.* He was, however, also a critic of music, dance, drama, and politics. He was awarded the Nobel Prize for Literature in 1925. In the extract for Hedda Gabler, Shaw discusses Hedda's drives and desires.]

Hedda is intensely curious about the side of life which is forbidden to her, and in which powerful instincts, absolutely ignored and condemned in her circle, steal their satisfaction. An odd intimacy springs up between the inquisitive girl and the rake. Whilst the general reads the paper in the afternoon, Lovborg and Hedda have long conversations in which he describes to her all his disreputable adventures. Although she is the questioner, she never dares to trust him: all the questions are indirect; and the responsibility for his interpretations rests on him alone. Hedda has no conviction whatever that these conversations are disgraceful; but she will not risk a fight with society on the point: it is easier to practise hypocrisy, the homage that truth pays to falsehood, than to endure ostracism. When he proceeds to make advances to her, Hedda has again no conviction that it would be wrong for her to gratify his instinct and her own; so that she is confronted with the alternative of sinning against herself and him, or sinning against social ideals in which she has no faith. Making the coward's choice, she carries it out with the utmost bravado, threatening Lovborg with one of her father's pistols, and driving him out of the house with all that ostentation of outraged purity which is the instinctive defence of women to whom chastity is not natural, much as libel actions are mostly brought by persons concerning whom libels are virtually, if not technically, justifiable.

Hedda, deprived of her lover, now finds that a life of conformity without faith involves something more terrible than the utmost ostracism: to wit, boredom. This scourge, unknown among revolutionists, is the curse which makes the security of respectability as dust in the balance against the unflagging interest of rebellion, and which forces society to eke out its harmless resources for killing time by licensing gambling, gluttony, hunting, shooting, coursing, and other vicious distractions for which even idealism has no disguise. These licenses, being expensive, are available only for people who have more than enough money to keep up appearances; and as Hedda's father, being in the army instead of in commerce, is too poor to leave her much more than the pistols, her boredom is only mitigated by dancing, at which she gains much admiration, but no substantial offers of marriage.

At last she has to find somebody to support her. A good-natured mediocrity of a professor is the best that is to be had; and though she regards him as a member of an inferior class, and despises almost to loathing his family circle of two affectionate old aunts and the inevitable general servant who has helped to bring him up, she marries him *faute de mieux*, and immediately proceeds to wreck this prudent provision for her livelihood by accommodating his income to her expenditure instead of accommodating her expenditure to his income. Her nature so rebels against the whole sordid transaction that the prospect of bearing a child to her husband drives her almost frantic, since it will not only expose her to the intimate solicitude of his aunts in the course of a derangement of her health in which she can see nothing that is not repulsive and humiliating, but will make her one of his family in earnest.

To amuse herself in these galling circumstances, she forms an underhand alliance with a visitor who belongs to her old set, an elderly gallant who quite understands how little she cares for her husband, and proposes a *ménage à trois* to her. She consents to his coming there and talking to her as he pleases behind her husband's back; but she keeps her pistols in reserve in case he becomes seriously importunate.

—George Bernard Shaw, *The Quintessence of Ibsenism* (New York: Hill and Wang, 1957): 109–111.

CAROLINE W. MAYERSON ON MOCK TRAGEDY

[Caroline W. Mayerson is a professor of English at Newcomb College in New Orleans. In this excerpt, Mayerson discusses the "mock-tragedy" quality of Hedda Gabler.]

Her inability to perceive the difference between melodrama and tragedy accounts for the disparity between Hedda's presumptive view of her own suicide and our evaluation of its significance. Ibsen with diabolical irony arranged a situation which bears close superficial resemblance to the traditional tragic end. Symbolically withdrawing herself from the bourgeois environment into the inner chamber which contains the reliques of her earlier life, Hedda plays a "wild dance" upon her piano and, beneath her father's portrait, shoots herself "beautifully" through the temple with her father's pistol. She dies to vindicate her heritage of independence; with disciplined and direct aim she at last defeats the Boyg, which hitherto she has unsuccessfully attempted to circumvent. So Hedda would see her death, we are led to believe, could she be both principal and spectator; and no doubt she would find high-sounding phrases with which to memorialize it. But of course it is Brack and Tesman who have the curtain lines, and these lines show how little of her intent Hedda has conveyed to her world. And we, having the opportunity to judge the act with relation to its full context, may properly interpret it as the final self-dramatization of the consistently sterile protagonist. Hedda gains no insight; her death affirms nothing of importance. She never understands why, at her touch, everything becomes "ludicrous and mean." She dies to escape a sordid situation that is largely of her own making; she will not face reality nor assume responsibility for the consequences of her acts. The pistols, having descended to a coward and a cheat, bring only death without honor. ⟨. . .⟩

⟨T⟩he characters, like those in the other plays of Ibsen's last period, are the living dead who dwell in a waste-land that resembles T. S. Eliot's. And, like Eliot later, Ibsen emphasized the aridity of the present by contrasting with the heroic past. Indeed, *Hedda Gabler* may be thought of as a mock-tragedy, a sardonically contrived travesty of tragic action, which Ibsen shows us is no longer possible in the world of the play. This world is sick with a disease less curable than that of Oedipus' Thebes or Hamlet's Denmark. For its hereditary leaders are shrunken in stature, maimed and paralyzed by their enslavement to the ideals of the dominant middle-class. With the other hollow men, they despise but nonetheless worship the false gods of respectability and security, paying only lip-service to their ancestral principles. Such geniuses as this society produces are, when left to themselves, too weak to do more than batter their own heads against constricting barriers. They dissipate their talents and so fail in their mission as prophets and disseminators of western culture; its interpretation is left to the unimaginative pedant, picking over the dry bones of the past. ⟨. . .⟩ And appropriately holding the center of the stage throughout is Hedda, in whom the shadows of the past still struggle in a losing battle with the sterile specter of the present. Her pistols are engraved with the insignia which the others understand not at all and which she only dimly comprehends. Her colossal egotism, her lack of self-knowledge, her cowardice, render her search for fulfillment but a succession of futile blunders which culminate in the supreme futility of death. Like Peer Gynt, she is fit only for the ladle of the button-molder; she fails to realize a capacity either for great good or for great evil. Her mirror-image wears the mask of tragedy, but Ibsen makes certain that we see the horns and pointed ears of the satyr protruding from behind it.

—Caroline W. Mayerson, "Thematic Symbols in *Hedda Gabler.*" In *Ibsen: A Collection of Critical Essays*, ed. Rolf Fjelde (Englewood Cliffs, N.J.: Prentice-Hall, 1965): 137–138.

Stephen Whicher on Ibsen's Characters

[Stephen Whicher was professor of English at Cornell University specializing in American literature and modern drama. He was also the author of *Freedom and Fate: An Inner Life of Ralph Waldo Emerson* and co-editor of the anthology *Twelve American Poets*. In this excerpt Whicher discusses the restlessness and pessimism of Ibsen's characters.]

The same violent rebellion at man's damnable littleness lies at the heart of Ibsen's first "modern" plays: *Pillars of Society, A Doll's House, Ghosts,* and *An Enemy of the People.* All are blows against the petty forces in society that hinder man from obeying the motto taught in *Peer Gynt*: Be Thyself. Nora's challenge to society, for instance, is still Brand's, transferred from a Herculean figure to the least likely of persons, as if to stress its necessity to all men. When she ceases to be her husband's doll and sets out to be herself, she also must sacrifice children, reputation, all she has of value. She must give all or nothing. ⟨. . .⟩

The same pessimistic skepticism controls the next three plays, varied as they are. *The Lady from the Sea*, the most "positive" and the slightest of the three, reads like a companion piece to *A Doll's House*. Wisely released by her husband, Ellida sees the folly of a desperate plunge like Nora's into the unknown, and freely chooses home and responsibility. In *Rosmersholm* the ruthless woman of action Fru Alving wished to be is broken by the ghost of the past as much as is the innocent idealist and dreamer; the dead wife claims them both. The divine discontent of Brand and the young Peer dwindles in *Hedda Gabler* to a sick restlessness, purely aimless and destructive. The cold dissection of the human animal in that most mirthless of comedies finds its spokesman in Hetman, the Brendel of the first draft of *Rosmersholm*: "The Master forgot to give us wings. Both outer and inner ones. So let us crawl on the earth as long as we can. There is nothing else to be done."

The hard detachment of *Hedda Gabler* masked Ibsen's own deep involvement. As the acid of skepticism ate inward, past the "Christian" condemnation of Brand and the general verdict on mankind of these later plays, it revealed the true pattern etched on the plate: Ibsen's personal guilt. He had charity for Peer, none for himself. He held Doomsday over himself in the four introspective plays of his old age, beginning with *The Master Builder*. What had the great work amounted to, each play asks over again, to which he had sacrificed so much? "Nothing, nothing! The whole is nothing." And the price! Happiness, love, life itself, and not his only but that of others as well.

Solness feels the thought of what he has done to those who loved him as "a great raw place here on my breast" that will never heal. The lure of the heights, as Allmers discovered, is the lure of death; and Borkman and Rubek finally discover that they *are* dead, self-slain.

The last plays have been called dramas of redemption, but surely no bubble of hope was ever more fragile than the castles in the air that the heroes of these plays dream of. The dominant image in them, one might well say in all Ibsen's drama, is the wide eyes of the dead children—all the sacrificed lives, including his own. "It is not true," Rita tells Allmers after the drowning and little Eyolf, "that he was swept away at once. They say they saw him lying on the bottom. Deep down in the clear water. They say he lay on his back. Quite still. With great open eyes. . . ." "And now we shall never, never see him again." "Day and night I shall see him before me as he lay there. With great open eyes."

—Stephen Whicher, "The World of Ibsen." In *Ibsen: A Collection of Critical Essays*, ed. Rolf Fjelde (Englewood Cliffs, N.J.: Prentice-Hall, 1965): 171–172.

JANET GARTON ON HEDDA'S JEALOUSY

[Janet Garton, Senior Lecturer in Scandinavian Studies at the University of East Anglia, has edited *Facets of European Modernism*, a critical study of Jens Bjorneboe, and *Norwegian Women's Writing 1850–1990*. In this excerpt Garton discusses Hedda's intense jealousy and what it means to be "trollish."]

⟨Hedda⟩ has internalized the repressions of her society, and her exaggerated fear of scandal renders her incapable of defying public opinion. All she can do is to achieve her aims vicariously. Tesman has shown himself to be too lightweight to carry the burden of her ambitions, so she turns to Løvborg. This is why the competition with Thea becomes so fierce; Løvborg is to realize Hedda's dreams, and she cannot bear the thought that silly little Thea has inspired him. She is jealous of the new book, and when Løvborg suggests that the book is the child of his union with Thea, her hatred of it is intensified by and intensifies her hatred of the unwanted child she is carrying. As she burns the book at the end of Act III, she is no longer sure whether it is the book or the child she is destroying. ⟨. . .⟩ ('Now I'm burning your child, Thea! You with the curly hair! Your and Eilert Løvborg's child. Now I'm burning . . . I'm burning the child.' My translation; the Oxford Ibsen renders the last sentence as 'I'm burning *your* child,' which obscures the fact that Hedda is not just talking about Thea's child but widening the reference to include her own.) Ironically, she not only fails to inspire Løvborg either to live or to die in accordance with her ideals, but even loses the despised Tesman at the end to the influence of a woman she thought she could twist round her little finger.

By the end of the play, all her outlets are sealed off. Løvborg is gone, the baby is coming, and Tesman is gravitating towards Thea, who will fit effortlessly into the cosy group with Miss Tesman and Berthe. Only Brack is still drawn to her, but the playful badinage of their earlier relationship has been transformed into a sexual blackmail which he makes brutally clear he will exploit to the hilt. Mother and mistress are the roles left to her, roles with no power in the world that interests her. Geographically she is squeezed off the stage, and all that is left to her is one pistol. The one act of defiance she can perform is an act of self-destruction, a pitiful parody of the glorious self-assertion of which she had dreamed.

At the same time as Ibsen was writing *Hedda Gabler*, Jonas Lie, another of the 'four greats' of Norwegian literature's Golden Age, was composing a book of tales entitled *Trolls* (1891). In the introduction, he explained what he understood by that word: 'That there are trolls in people is understood by anyone who has an eye for such things . . . Troll magic lives . . . within people in the form of temperament, natural will, explosiveness . . . And how far this troll stage follows mankind further into civilized society, would be a useful and instructive study, possibly also a somewhat surprising one.' Like Ibsen, Lie was aware that trolls and the like were not just decorative national symbols but an expression of an intuitive understanding of the forces that determine people's actions and cannot be explained in terms of logic and rationality, the forces that are hidden away from the daylight. What Ibsen is doing in the plays I have looked at could be defined as an investigation of the way in which 'the troll stage' has followed mankind into civilized society. His central characters are driven to the brink of self-destruction, and sometimes beyond, by conflicts between conscious and subconscious drives.

—Janet Garton, "The Middle Plays." In *The Cambridge Companion to Ibsen*, ed. James McFarlane (Cambridge: Cambridge University Press, 1994): 122–123.

Vigdis Ystad on Eilert Løvborg

[Vigdis Ystad teaches in the Department of Scandinavian Studies at the University of Oslo. He is currently joint editor of the biennial *Contemporary Approaches to Ibsen*. In this excerpt, Ystad discusses Eilert Løvborg's role in *Hedda Gabler*.]

Ejlert Løvborg ⟨. . .⟩ was once a scholar of considerable promise. His career was interrupted because of alcohol abuse, but now he is restored to health and has just published a scholarly book that by far surpasses anything Hedda's spouse could hope to produce. Jørgen Tesman is preoccupied with the dead remnants of the past—specifically, Brabantian domestic industry in the Middle Ages (mostly a lace industry), whereas Ejlert is now writing about something as visionary as the cultural development of the future.

The two men are depicted as contrasts, and there is no doubt where Hedda's sympathies lie. In her younger days, she had had daring conversations with Ejlert. These conversations revolved around eroticism and a life freely expressed, consequently around alternatives to the mode of life characteristic of the conventional Victorian society in which Hedda lives. But the attraction to Ejlert is not only of the erotic kind. He is also intellectually far more attractive than the lacemonger Jørgen Tesman.

From this perspective, we can understand Hedda's dream of restoring Ejlert to what he *was*. For in this way, he can actualize the dreams that she carries within her, dreams for which she has no words. She says that he shall be resurrected for her sake with "vine leaves in his hair". He shall emerge as a Dionysan god—but without succumbing to new orgies of alcohol and sexuality. At the same time, he shall retain his intellectual self, his self-control and self-command—that is, aspects of his personality that might properly be called Apollonian. And Ejlert is to be instrumental in transforming Hedda's existence. He shall be both Dionysus and Apollo, both lush self-expression and lucid consciousness. In other words, he shall create something *new* by incorporating his erotic as well as his intellectual vigour into the universal. The *new* dimension is that he becomes himself as the one he *was*—in becoming revealed, that is, in disclosing himself. That is Hedda's dream for the future—and perhaps it is also Ejlert's.

We know that Hedda's project fails. She provokes the recovered alcoholic into participating in a drinking party with Tesman and Brack. She believes that he will have enough self-control to manage the Dionysian ecstasy. But that is not to be. Ejlert ends up in the establishment of Miss Diana, the prostitute, where he shoots himself by accident. A bullet penetrates his abdomen, and he dies. He was not able to break out of his hiddenness, step into the open, and integrate his hiddenness in the society of the future.

But what about Hedda? She does what she had demanded of Ejlert. She unites passion and self-control, putting a bullet through her temple. When her great dream collapses—the dream of having Ejlert change the world so as to make room for eros—everything unconscious and pagan also collapses. There remains only one way out for her to bring her ideals into the open and make them visible. It is the same way chosen by Hjørdis, namely, suicide.

> —Vigdis Ystad, "Ibsen's Rebellious Women." In *Ibsen at the Centre for Advanced Study*, ed. Vigdis Ystad (Oslo: Scandinavian University Press, 1997): 148–149.

HELGE RØNNING ON IBSEN AND EUROPEAN POLITICS

[Helge Rønning teaches in the Department of Media and Communication at the University of Oslo. In this excerpt, Rønning discusses the social upheaval permeating Europe during the time of Ibsen, and Ibsen's own position within the political scene.]

The 1870s were, from a European perspective, clearly perceived as a period of transition. Its lines of development were uneven. While economic conditions could be advanced, the political system and ideological and religious ideas might be less so. Some areas of European countries were well developed, while others did not seem to have changed noticeably since the Middle Ages. A country typical of this was Italy, partly due to the disparities between its northern and southern regions. During Ibsen's stay in Rome, Italy was undergoing a political modernization process culminating in the city's becoming the capital of a unified Italian nation in 1871. ⟨. . .⟩

In the early 1870s, an extremely significant political event occurred, an event which in many ways was to become a symbol of an effort to bring history into a new phase. The early labour movement saw it as a sign of coming revolution; the liberal bourgeoisie interpreted it as a need to ally itself with more conservative forces. For the radical intellectuals it created a dilemma. In many ways, they were in a situation that had no answer. Preferring both harmony and radical change, they appeared to opt for the utopian solution. The event referred to, needless to say, is the Paris Commune. Several references to the dilemma facing it appeared in the correspondence between Ibsen and Georg Brandes during the 1870s. Brandes, who with his 1871 lecture on emigrant literature came to be seen as a spokesman for the radicalism of the Commune, repeatedly returned to the problem in his later writing.

With the conception of a utopian liberalism in mind, Ibsen, on the one hand, castigates the type of radicalism which had given into the realities of the bourgeoisie while, on the other, strongly criticizing the type of idealism which had lost touch with reality. His work constantly deals with the way in which values, according to the ideals of a true and heroic liberalism, become tarnished in adjusting to a restrictive and narrow bourgeois society. Values professed by a heroic liberalism and tarnished by a practical liberalism comprise belief in truth, love, equality among free and independent individuals, rational and critical thinking, and artistic beauty.

Together with Brandes, Ibsen, who shared his ideas, appears as one seeking to preserve liberal ideals. It was a period when society, professing liberalism in name only, distanced itself from the ideals of liberty, equality, and truth, proving to be a society of injustice, inequality, and hypocrisy. Ibsen, Brandes, and other true radical liberalists defended "non-realizable" ideals, even if they sometimes appeared to be inconsistent in their thinking. ⟨. . .⟩

Ibsen's plays present a picture of the mind and of the senses incompatible with the conception of a strong and undivided society. The question that invariably emerges is whether society itself is divided, terror-ridden, contradictory, and unpredictable, or this holds only for individual people. The plays also raise questions about what kind of society produces such maladjusted people as those moving around in the rooms of the various stage sets, readily taken for the real homes of the bourgeoisie, and the characters that emerge as reflections of the audience watching them.

For Ibsen, individual freedom was the essential issue. He was not really concerned with social freedom, even though it could be argued that he saw the one as a condition for the other. What he shows us in his plays are the forces opposing individual freedom, preventing liberation. The plays are concerned with the individual wishing to liberate himself from an artificial position of compromise, and struggling for insight and independence. This very process which crushes the will for freedom and independence is what Ibsen examines. Usually, it results in the destruction of the individual, or at least in unfulfilled goals, and an individual bereft of illusions.

> —Helge Rønning, "The Unconscious Evil of Idealism and the Liberal Dilemma, An Analysis of Thematic Structures in *Emperor and Galilean* and *The Wild Duck*." In *Ibsen, at the Centre for Advanced Study*, ed. Vigdis Ystad (Oslo: Scandinavian University Press, 1997): 171–175.

Plot Summary of
The Master Builder

Halvard Solness is a successful and revered architect who drives his staff of three mercilessly, to the point of cruelty. Among them is Knut Brovik, an architect who once had Solness in *his* employ, but now Solness owns him as well as Brovik's son, Ragnar, and Ragnar's fiancé, Kaja Fosli. Knut is old and dying and his one wish is to see his son Ragnar get a chance to design his own buildings and set out on his own. Knut begs Solness to give Ragnar just one of his commissions, but Solness refuses. He confesses that he is afraid of youth just as he is afraid of change.

Solness tells Kaja, the frail young bookkeeper, that it is not Ragnar he is desperate to retain but Kaja herself and that he fears if Ragnar goes, she will leave also. Kaja is mesmerized by this man of great power, and when he tells her he cannot be without her, she even proposes ridding herself of her fiancé. Though Solness expresses his need to her, what he conveys is not love but a cold and disturbing domination over her mind and soul. Solness even confesses to the family doctor and confidant, Herdal, that he seems to have a strange telepathic power over her.

Solness has become a sordid mess of a man over the years, willing to exploit anyone who can help him achieve artistic success, and he has dragged his wife down with him. Solness knows this and is plagued with guilt.

Into this poisonous atmosphere comes a youthful stranger, Hilda Wangel. Her arrival is seemingly an answer to Solness's wishes. Though he fears youth, he craves it. Hilda's visit is prompted by a promise he had made her ten years previous, to the day, to build her a castle and make her a princess. She declares she has come for her castle. She reminds him about a party held in his honor at the dedication of his church tower at Lysanger. There he cornered her in a room and kissed her—she could not have been more than thirteen. But it was a climb Solness made to the top of the tower he built with his own hands that Hilda remembers with most rapture, as he placed a celebratory wreath on the weather vane.

Solness is captivated by Hilda, and takes her into his confidence. He confesses to her the source of his greatest guilt: he left a crack in his own chimney unattended several years ago in secret, even subconscious, hope that the house would burn, giving him a chance to clear the estate his parents-in-law had given them and build on it, new homes for happy families. But the fire killed his two baby boys, and Aline, his wife, has been mourning ever since. Solness is afraid that he willed the fire to happen. To repent, Solness is building another home for Aline and himself. This house will have an exultant tower, like that of a church.

When Hilda speaks with Aline alone on a verandah, Hilda discovers that Aline's mourning is less about the children she lost than about the things her parents left her that were destroyed in the fire—particularly nine dolls. This disturbing incongruity is lost on Solness who believes her to be mourning those baby boys.

The new house is nearly complete and Hilda is determined to see her master builder climb to the top once again, see her hero ascend to his "castle in the air." What she doesn't know is that the only time he was ever able to overcome his terror of heights and climb the tower was ten years ago at Lysanger. But she begs him and urges him higher and higher—until he falls, and dies. And yet Hilda is triumphant: Her master builder went straight to the top.

Throughout the play we see that Solness is a tormented man, one who has paid a great price for his triumphs: his wife's happiness, his staff's, and his own. He senses that he is split within, that his artistic will is greater than any other. It's this other will which again is identified with the troll—that devilish imp, both playful and malevolent. The inner-troll drives him, pushing him both away from humanity and toward higher achievement. Now he is a man in crisis. Solness's fears have overtaken him at last, his conscience has choked him, and his muse has left him.

Hilda appears suddenly as a cathartic, renewing presence, a reflection of himself and his inner-troll, but most significantly, as the instigator of that final frenzied rush toward the holy grail of artistic success—"castles in the air." When Hilda says to him, "I want my kingdom. Time's up," it could just as well be him saying it to himself.

Solness tells her, "You're like a dawning day. When I look at you—then it's as if I looked into the sunrise." He is clearly in need of rejuvenation, and it is youth that can do it for him, though he knows what youth means for him—death. Youth will establish itself, and the old will die out. Solness craves the experience of youthful originality and simultaneously fears it:

SOLNESS: . . . all these years I've been going around tormented by— hmm—

HILDA: By what?

SOLNESS: By a search for something—some old experience I thought I'd forgotten. But I've never had an inkling of what it could be.

Solness was the nearest to a self-portrait that Ibsen would try. He admitted in an address to the students of Christiania six years later that Solness was "a man somewhat akin to me." Ibsen had also long considered himself a builder of plays which were like architecture. In a poem written in his youth, "Building Plan," he had compared the artist to a master builder. Ibsen even had a terrible fear of heights as did Solness.

Ibsen also wanted to explore the idea of hypnosis in *The Master Builder* as he did in the three previous plays. Interest in hypnosis was becoming widespread in Europe right at this time. Sigmund Freud had already used it therapeutically and many prominent thinkers would write about it. Ibsen was interested in the general idea of one person's ability to control the mind of another, rather than strict hypnosis. Solness, for example, is able to gain control over the minds of Kaja, Hilda, and to some extent, his "helpers and servers" as he calls them, meaning all those who enable him to be what he is. His unexpressed desires become the actions of others, much to his own amazement.

When Hilda arrives suddenly, he believes it was a subconscious yearning which brought her. Hilda gives him an account of their first meeting which happened ten years previous to the day. She reminds him of the kiss he gave her, of the promise he made, and, most importantly, of his climb to the top of the tower. For her, watching him climb to the top of the church tower was an ecstatic experience and she has come to repeat it. Solness does not remember the kiss or the promise, but is gradually led to the memory. We cannot be sure that it actually happened, but it hardly matters. This is what Hilda believes, and what Solness comes to remember. Solness quickly takes her into his ring of "servers and helpers." She is releasing him and his pent-up creative energies. In short, she is a new muse. When Solness offers her a job, she refuses it, thus aligning herself with things of the spirit and asserting her apparitional presence.

Solness directs his wife, Aline, to allow Hilda a residence in one of the empty nurseries, where the memories of the dead children are lingering. Aline dutifully complies. Solness's long-suffering wife is one of Solness's victims, and yet she is not against him. She is resentful of his string of female admirers, but she still holds him in high regard as he does her. Ibsen said, "Solness and his wife are worthy people who don't suit each other and so aren't happy in their life together. They don't become what, being the people they are, they could and should have become—despite the fact that they aren't actually miserable, and despite their consideration for each other and a kind of tenderness and love." They have, to some degree, driven each other mad. Herdal, the family doctor is alerted to the fragile sanity of both Solness and Aline, each by the other. We are aware throughout the play, of Solness's maniacal tendencies, and are then prepared when the capricious Hilda pushes him over the edge.

Ibsen was aware of a legend of a master builder who had built a church and had thrown himself down from the tower because he was afraid the roof would not hold. His friend Helene Raff told him that, in fact, many churches in Germany had that same legend and Ibsen replied that it must be because people felt instinctively that a man could not build so high without paying a price for his nearness to God. Hilda pushes Solness to try something even more presumptuous than high towers—castles in the air. Solness asks her what sort of castle she imagines for herself. "My castle must stand up—very high up—and free on every side. So I can see far—far out," she replies. Later she names her castle a "castle in the air."

HILDA: (rising impatiently, with a scornful gesture of her hand)
             Why, yes, of course! Castles in the air—they're so easy to hide
             away in. And easy to build too. (Looking contemptuously at
             him.) Especially for builders who have a—dizzy conscience.
SOLNESS: (getting up) From this day on we'll build together, Hilda.
HILDA   (with a skeptical smile) A real castle in the air?
SOLNESS: Yes. One with solid foundations.

When Hilda finally gets her way and Solness attempts the climb to the top of his new home, meant for himself and Aline, she is exultant: "At last! At last! Now I can see him great and free again."

Despite the seemingly secret language in which Solness and Hilda speak, Ibsen was dismayed at the variety of symbols the audience usually ascribed to his work. He asserted that he wrote merely about the inner life of real people. *The Master Builder* is fundamentally about an overwrought old artist toward the end of his creativity, searching and yearning for youth, that is, searching for redemption.

HILDA: What did you want from me?
SOLNESS: You, Hilda, are youth.
HILDA: (smiles) Youth, that you're so afraid of?
SOLNESS: (nodding slowly) And that, deep within me, I'm so much
          hungering for. ❀

List of Characters in
The Master Builder

Halvard Solness is a successful, driven architect who has destroyed his own happiness and that of his wife to win the battles he has. He is plagued with guilt for it, but is driven still further by a young woman, Hilda Wangel, who declares she wants a castle he promised her ten years ago.

Aline Solness is Halvard's long-suffering wife. She is only one of the many victim's of his ambition and while she is fond of him, she doesn't ever willingly occupy the same room with him. She is dressed always in black, since a fire years previous caused the death of her twin babies.

Dr. Herdal is the family doctor and confidant. Both Aline and Solness have alerted him to the fragile sanity of the other, and he is on careful lookout for signs of instability in both.

Knut Brovik is the old man in Solness's employ who was once an architect in his own right but lost his business and is now under the power of Solness. His one wish before he dies is that his son Ragnar would be able to strike out on his own and build his own houses rather than remain under Solness.

Ragnar Brovik is Knut Brovik's son. He is also in the employ of Solness and has been yearning to get commissions of his own. Solness will not have it, however, and refuses to encourage him in any way.

Kaja Fosli is Solness's bookkeeper and Ragnar's fiancé. Since she came to be employed by Solness, he has gained an ever stronger hold on her mind. She both loves and fears Solness and so is his emotional captive, willing even to leave Ragnar for him.

Hilda Wangel is a young woman from Lysanger, who arrives unexpectedly at Solness's house demanding a castle he promised her ten years ago when she was thirteen. He called her a princess and said he would give her a kingdom when she was grown. Though his offer was not made seriously, she appears to be quite in earnest. ❀

Critical Views on
The Master Builder

GEORGE BERNARD SHAW ON THE ARCHITECT'S SACRIFICE

[George Bernard Shaw (1856–1950) is best known as a playwright of such plays as *Pygmalion, Heartbreak House,* and *Three Plays for Puritans.* He was, however, also a critic of music, dance, drama, and politics. He was awarded the Nobel Prize for Literature in 1925. In the extract for *The Master Builder,* Shaw discusses what Solness has sacrificed in himself and in others to be the architect he is.]

The fire did not come from the crack in the chimney when all the domestic fires were blazing. It came at night when the fires were low, and began in a cupboard quite away from the chimney. It came when Mrs. Solness and the children were in bed. It shattered the mother's health; it killed the children she was nursing; it devoured the portraits and the silk dresses and the old lace; it burnt the nine lovely dolls; and it broke the heart under which the dolls had lain like little unborn children. That was the price of the woman; and he is trying to atone by building her a new villa: a new tomb to replace the old home; for he is gnawed with remorse.

But the fire was not only a good building speculation: it also led to his obtaining commissions to build churches. And one triumphant day, when he was celebrating the completion of the giant tower he had added to the old church at Lysanger, it suddenly flashed on him that his house had been burnt, his wife's life laid waste, and his own happiness destroyed, so that he might become a builder of churches. Now it happens that one of his difficulties as a builder is that he had a bad head for heights, and cannot venture even on a second floor balcony. Yet in the fury of that thought he mounts to the pinnacle of his tower, and there, face to face with God, who has, he feels, wasted the wife's gift of building up the souls of little children to make the husband a builder of steeples, he declares that he will never set hand to church-building again, and will henceforth build nothing but homes for happier men than he. Which vow he keeps, only to find that the home, too, is a devouring idol, and that men and women have no longer any use for it.

In spite of his excitement, he very nearly breaks his neck after all; for among the crowd below there is a little devil of a girl who waves a white scarf and makes his head swim. This tiny animal is no other than the younger stepdaughter of Ellida, The Lady from the Sea, Hilda Wangel, of whose taste for "thrilling" sensations we had a glimpse in that play. On the same evening Solness is entertained at a club banquet, in consequence of which he is not in the most responsible condition when he returns to sup at the house of Dr. Wangel, who is putting him up for the night. He meets the imp there; thinks her like a little princess in her white dress; kisses her; and promises her to come back in ten years and carry her off to the kingdom of Orangia. Perhaps it is only just to mention that he stoutly denies these indiscretions afterwards; though he admits that when he wishes something to happen between himself and somebody else, the somebody else always imagines it actually has happened.

The play begins ten years after the climbing of the tower. The younger generation knocks at the door with a vengeance. Hilda, now a vigorous young woman, and a great builder of castles in the air, bursts in on him and demands her kingdom; and very soon she sends him up to a tower again (the tower of the new house) and waves her scarf to him as madly as ever. This time he really does break his neck; and so the story ends.

—George Bernard Shaw, *The Quintessence of Ibsenism* (New York: Hill and Wang, 1957): 121–123.

E. M. FORSTER ON BITTERNESS IN IBSEN'S PLAYS

[E. M. Forster (1879–1970) is best known for his novels such as *A Passage to India* and *Howard's End*. He also published collections of essays such as *Abinger Harvest* and *Two Cheers for Democracy*. Here Forster discusses the pervasive quality of bitterness in Ibsen's plays.]

Seldom can a great genius have had so large a dose of domestic irritability. ⟨Ibsen⟩ was cross with his enemies and friends, with theater-managers, professors, and students, and so cross with his countrymen for not volunteering to help the Danes in 1864 that he had to go to Italy to say so. He might have volunteered in person—he was in the prime of life at the time—but this did not occur to him; he preferred instead to write a scathing little satire about a Norwegian mother whose son was safe at the front. And it is (if one may adopt the phrase) precisely the volunteer spirit that is absent from his conception of human relationships. He put everything into them except the strength of his arm.

"Not a great writer . . . almost great, but marred by this lack of generosity." How readily the phrases rise to the lips! How false they are! For this nagging quality, this habitual bitterness—they are essential in his greatness, because they beckon to the poetry in him, and carry it with them under the ground. Underground. Into the depths of the sea, the depths of the sea. Had he been of heroic build and turned to the light and the sun, his gifts would have evaporated. But he was—thank heaven—subterranean, he loved narrow passages and darkness, and his later plays have a romantic intensity which not only rivals the romantic expansion of their predecessors, but is absolutely unique in literature. The trees in old Ekdal's aviary are as numerous as a forest because they are countless, the water in the chickens' trough includes all the waves on which the Vikings could sail. To his impassioned vision dead and damaged things, however contemptible socially, dwell for ever in the land of romance, and this is the secret of his so-called symbolism: a connection is found between objects that lead different types of existence; they reinforce one another and each lives more intensely than before. Consequently his stage throbs with a mysteriousness for which no obvious preparation has been made, with beckonings, tremblings, sudden compressions of the air, and his characters as they wrangle among the oval tables and stoves are watched by an unseen power which slips between their words.

A weaker dramatist who had this peculiar gift would try to get his effect by patches of fine writing, but with Ibsen as with Beethoven the beauty comes not from the tunes, but from the way they are used and are worked into the joints of the action. *The Master Builder* contains superb examples of this. The plot unfolds logically, the diction is flat and austere, the scene is a villa close to which another villa is being erected, the chief characters are an elderly couple and a young woman who is determined to get a thrill out of her visit, even if it entails breaking her host's neck. Hilda is a minx, and though her restlessness is not so vulgar as Hedda Gabler's it is quite as pernicious and lacks the saving gesture of suicide. That is one side of Hilda. But on the other side she touches Gerd and the Rat-Wife and the Button-molder, she is a lure and an assessor, she comes from the non-human and asks for her kingdom and for castles in the air that shall rest on solid masonry, and from the moment she knocks at the door poetry filters into the play.

—E. M. Forster, "Ibsen the Romantic." In *Ibsen: A Collection of Critical Essays*, ed. Rolf Fjelde (Englewood Cliffs, N.J.: Prentice-Hall, 1965): 175–177.

BRIAN W. DOWNS ON HILDA

[Brian W. Downs, Master of Christ's College and Professor of Scandinavian Studies in the University of Cambridge, has written several books on Ibsen including *A Study of Six Plays by Ibsen*. In this study, Downs discusses the character of Hilda and her dramatic purpose.]

Solness appears to have made some professional reputation quite quickly, since he received the commission to build the church tower at Lysanger, a place remote from his home. It was just a little after the time that his great opportunity had come to him: his wife's old home had burned down and, as with it the reason for leaving intact the large estate round it had disappeared, it was broken up into building plots on which Solness put up the 'homes for men and women' that had made him the most successful man, locally, in his profession. The set-up of his drawing office—two rooms, it seems, in his own house and a staff of two men and a girl—forbids us to picture him as an architect of outstanding eminence, but in the circumstances of a comparatively small community, he is obviously much sought after and financially as prosperous as he could wish. His home-life, however, is unhappy. The accident to which he owed his prosperity involved the death of his two children and the sterility of his wife Aline: his wife's mind, too, has sustained a grave injury, though there are no grounds for thinking it actually deranged.

Not unconnected with this half of the *donnée* is the other. For it was on completing the church tower at Lysanger, when Solness finally decided to devote himself to domestic architecture, that he had first encountered Hilda Wangel. So intoxicated with that decision and the convivial celebrations following on the inauguration of the tower that the episode quite passed out of his mind, he had taken her, then a little girl of twelve or thirteen, into his arms, kissed her over and over again and promised in ten years' time to make her a princess and give her a kingdom.

The actual drama of *The Master Builder* begins in the evening of this anniversary day with the sudden and completely unexpected arrival in the Solness house of Hilda Wangel, insistent on the execution of the promise Halvard Solness had made her. Before her entry, there have been two scenes of exposition (in which the prehistories are scarcely glanced at). They show that not everything is well with the outwardly prosperous, well-balanced architect Halvard Solness, who is both 'at the head of his profession' and in the prime of life. First, they draw attention to the kind of tyranny which he exercises over his small staff: attached to his service he has a decayed architect Brovik, and Brovik's son Ragnar, who are extremely useful to him in certain branches of his vocation which he does not seem to have mastered himself, and he is determined to keep them even by illegitimate means; one influence over them he exercises through his clerk, Kaja Fosli, Ragnar Brovik's *fiancée*, who is slavishly devoted to her employer and whose devotion he ensures by a show of affection which he does not really feel. Solness knows the whole situation to be thoroughly false and reprehensible, all the more so as his relation with Kaja obviously distresses his wife; but, as he explains to the physician and friend of the family, Dr Herdal, he welcomes the consequent pangs of remorse as 'salutary self-torture,' a form of expiation for the unhappiness which, on other grounds too, he has brought upon his wife; he feels, too, that some mysterious agency drives him along a certain line of conduct and that he must go on in his dealings with the Broviks and Kaja as he has begun. Further, the Broviks serve as a reminder and safeguard of what he most fears, his supersession by the younger generation.

With a striking *coup de théâtre*, upon the words 'Yes, just you see, doctor—presently the younger generation will come knocking at the door. . . . Then there's an end of Halvard Solness,' a knock is heard at the door and Hilda Wangel enters. Solness has not the least idea who she is, but the reintroduction is effected by Herdal, who met her during the recent summer holidays. Arrangements are made for Hilda to stay the night, and, left to themselves, she and Solness take up the remainder of the act with the reconstruction of the events of ten years ago, culminating in Hilda's demand to have the kingdom then promised her handed over at once and Solness's avowal '*You are the very being I have needed most*'. . . .

—Brian W. Downs, *A Study of Six Plays By Ibsen* (Cambridge: Cambridge University Press, 1950): 179–181.

ERIC BENTLEY ON REBELLIOUSNESS IN IBSEN'S PLAYS

[Eric Bentley is a literary critic and a translator and writer on theater. From 1953 to 1969 he was the Brandes-Matthews Professor of Dramatic Literature at Columbia University in New York. He has published numerous dramatic and critical works including *The Recantation of Galileo Galilei, The Playwright as Thinker, In Search of Theatre, The Theatre of Commitment,* and, as editor and translator, *Seven Plays by Bertold Brecht* and *Naked Masks by Priandello.* In this excerpt, Bentley discusses the essential quality of rebelliousness in all of Ibsen's plays.]

Ibsen's plays are *about* rebels—from Catiline to Brand and Julian, and from Lona Hessel and Nora Helmer to Hedda Gabler and John Gabrial Borkman—and we should not need to be told by Ibsen himself (as we were) that he wrote only of what he had lived through, for rebelliousness is not only the subject of the plays but the motive force. Anti-clericalism (as in the portrait of Manders and of the Dean in *Brand*) and political satire (as in *The League of Youth* or the characterization of the Mayor in *Brand*) are merely the most obtrusive signs of a mentality that was critical through and through. As we retreat in horror, disgust, or mere boredom from the idea of the writer as Official Mouthpiece, we come back to the old liberal conception, most signally represented in this century by André Gide: the writer as questioner, dissenter, challenger, trouble-maker, at war with his age, yet by that token standing for the best in his age and helping the age to understand itself. In Ibsen, as in Gide, we who live in a time of fake radicalism are confronted by a real radical.

In speaking of fake radicalism, I again have more than Communism in mind—more even than politics. I am thinking, for example, of all playwrights who are considered daring, and whose courage is rather light-heartedly connected by critics with that of Ibsen and Strindberg. As people these playwrights are often much more Bohemian than Ibsen, and something much more quickly identifiable as Daring is smeared over the whole surface of their plays, which deal with assorted neuroses not even mentionable in the theatre of Ibsen's day. But Ibsen is supposed to have given Daring its start in *Ghosts*.

The mistake here is to imagine that the subject of *Ghosts* is syphilis. Lucky for Ibsen that it isn't, as the medical science of the play is now quite obsolete! His daring was not a matter of bringing up repellent subjects, though it included that. It consisted in his genuinely radical attitude to life in general. It is at the heart of his writing, not merely on its surface.

—Eric Bentley, "Henrik Ibsen: A Personal Statement." In *Ibsen: A Collection of Critical Essays*, ed. Rolf Fjelde (Englewood Cliffs, N.J.: Prentice-Hall, 1965): 14–15.

ARTHUR MILLER ON CHANGE REVEALED BY IBSEN

[Arthur Miller is a working playwright, famous for such plays as *The Crucible* and *Death of a Salesman*. Here Miller discusses the how Ibsen's plays reveal the ever-changing quality of life.]

There is one element in Ibsen's method which I do not think ought to be overlooked, let alone dismissed as it so often is nowadays. If his plays, and his method, do nothing else they reveal the evolutionary quality of life. One is constantly aware, in watching his plays, of process, change, development. I think too many modern plays assume, so to speak, that their duty is merely to show the present countenance rather than to account for what happens. It is therefore wrong to imagine that because his first and sometimes his second acts devote so much time to a studied revelation of antecedent material, his view is static compared to our own. In truth, it is profoundly dynamic, for that enormous past was always heavily documented to the end that the present be comprehended with wholeness, as a moment in a flow of time, and not—as with so many modern plays—as a situation without roots. Indeed, even though I can myself reject other aspects of his work, it nevertheless presents barely and unadorned what I believe is the biggest single dramatic problem, namely, how to dramatize what has gone before. I say this not merely out of technical interest, but because dramatic characters, and the drama itself, can never hope to attain a maximum degree of consciousness unless they contain a viable unveiling of the contrast between past and present, and an awareness of the process by which the present has become what it is. And I say this, finally, because I take it as a truth that the end of drama is the creation of a higher consciousness and not merely a subjective attack upon the audience's nerves and feelings. What is precious in the Ibsen method is its insistence upon valid causation, and this cannot be dismissed as a wooden notion.

This is the 'real' in Ibsen's realism for me, for he was, after all, as much a mystic as a realist. Which is simply to say that while there are mysteries in life which no amount of analyzing will reduce to reason, it is perfectly realistic to admit and even to proclaim that hiatus as a truth. But the problem is not to make complex what is essentially explainable; it is to make understandable what is complex without distorting and oversimplifying what cannot be explained. I think many of his devices are, in fact, quite arbitrary; that he betrays a Germanic ponderousness at times and a tendency to overprove what is quite clear in the first place. But we could do with more of his basic intention, which was to assert nothing he had not proved, and to cling always to the marvellous spectacle of life forcing one event out of the jaws of the preceding one and to reveal its elemental consistencies with surprise. In other words, I contrast his realism not with the lyrical, which I prize, but with sentimentality, which is always a leak in the dramatic dike. He sought to make a play as weighty and living a fact as the discovery of the steam engine or algebra. This can be scoffed away only at a price, and the price is a living drama.

—Arthur Miller, Introduction to *Collected Plays* (1957). Reprinted in *The Cambridge Companion to Ibsen*, ed. James McFarlane (Cambridge: Cambridge University Press, 1994): 127–128.

[Rolf Fjelde is a poet, playwright, scholar, and translator. His translations of Ibsen's plays have become standard. He currently teaches drama and film at Pratt Institute and the Julliard School in New York. In this extract, Fjelde discusses the difficulty that Ibsen's characters have finding a place for themselves in society.]

The theme of finding one's true vocation recurs throughout Ibsen's life and work, but its full importance is revealed only if seen as part of a larger problem: not merely a subjective quest for personal realization, but also an objective effort toward imaginative insight into the main tendencies of an age and a civilization. Again and again Ibsen's protagonists—Brand, Peer Gynt, Nora Helmer, Rosmer, Hedda Gabler, Solness—are shown as foundering on the dilemma of what to make of their lives in a society that is at least nominally open, the "little northern democracy" of Henry James's phrase; they do so as regularly and as symptomatically as, in a closed, if dissolving, late medieval society the Shakespearean tragic hero foundered on some transgression of fixed order and degree. Like "the heavens themselves, the planets and this center," the earth, Shakespeare's hero had his ordained place; it was given him *a priori* by the laws of nature and of nations, and the entire complex machinery of Shakespearean tragedy seems designed to demonstrate to him, at his own cost, that ignorance of the law is no excuse.

The Ibsen hero, on the other hand, neither knows his own place, nor has much reason to. The laws still exist, but their beautifully articulated order has broken apart; and he must discover or fail to discover, at his own cost, their various workings deep in his human nature. The method he employs in doing so, like the one the scientist uses in the arena of physical nature, is empirical and experimental—he closely observes himself, like Solness, and tests himself, like Hedda. In this condition of being thrown back on himself, he reflects the arrival, after a two hundred year timelag, of a kind of Cartesian doubt in the field of the drama. For the pressing question of the self and what to make of it, of which the theme of vocation is the most obvious expression, is simply the inward dimension of the objective predicament confronting the late nineteenth century man whose spiritual biography is written into the plays from *Brand* to *When We Dead Awaken.* ⟨. . .⟩

Born into a provincial milieu in an out-of-the-way corner of Europe, plunged into early poverty, deprived of an adequate education, presented with a hollow and outmoded national tradition whose praises he was expected to sing through the medium of an art at probably its lowest ebb in centuries, he had the intellect, the imagination, and the energy to turn these deficiencies into challenges; and the strengthening of talent that occurred through his progressive conquests of adversity served to carry him further and further in the consuming passion of his life, which was, in those several areas that concerned him most, to get to the root of things and build fresh and clean from a groundwork of truth.

Radical truth as the essential goal and guiding principle in life stands at the center of his achievement in the drama.

—Rolf Fjelde, Introduction to *Ibsen: A Collection of Critical Essays*, ed. Rolf Fjelde (Englewood Cliffs, N.J.: Prentice-Hall, 1965): 2–3.

MICHAEL MEYER ON SOLNESS

[Michael Meyer is a translator of Ibsen and Strindberg as well as a novelist and dramatist. He was lecturer in English Literature at Upsala University in Sweden until 1950 when he became a correspondent for the Swedish newspaper *Svenka Dagbladet*. In this excerpt from his biography on Ibsen, Meyer discusses Solness's lust for youth.]

Ibsen does not specify Solness's age—he merely called him "aging," probably to avoid too close an identification with himself—but he should surely be at least approaching sixty. Hilde is twenty-three; in other words, there should be not twenty, but nearly forty years between them; he should be old enough to be not merely her father but her grandfather. The theme of the play is an old man's fear of, and yearning for youth:

HILDE: What do you want from me?
SOLNESS: Your youth, Hilde.
HILDE: Youth, which you are so frightened of?
SOLNESS: (*nods slowly*) And which, in my heart, I long for.

"Oh, high and painful joy—to struggle for the unattainable!" Ibsen had written in Emilie's album three years earlier in Gossensass. But if we see a handsome man of fifty wooing a girl of thirty, the point is lost. Even when Solness is played by an actor who is in fact sixty, one has too often seen him age himself down to forty-five.

Another fault too often committed by actors playing Solness is a tendency to push him up the social scale. Solness has fought his way up; his way of speaking is rough, not the language of one socially sure of himself. He is socially inferior not merely to his wife, but also to Hilde (whose language, by contrast is immensely self-assured). Of course it is possible to argue that the son of "pious, country people" (as Solness describes himself) need not be, or feel, socially inferior to the daughter of a country doctor; what is certain is that the play gains immeasurably if the social difference is there, between Solness and Hilde as well as between Solness and Aline. And he must be played sensually; one has seen Solnesses who behaved as though they would have not known what to do if Hilde had started to take her clothes off.

The character of Solness was the nearest thing to a deliberate self-portrait that Ibsen had yet attempted (though he was to follow it with two equally merciless likenesses in *John Gabriel Borkman* and *When We Dead Awaken*). He admitted in an address to the students of Christiania six years later that Solness was "a man somewhat akin to me"; they shared an arrogancy and ruthlessness, a readiness to sacrifice the happiness of those close to them in order to further their ambitions, and that longing for and fear of youth. The sensuality was Ibsen's, too, inhibited though he was about giving rein to it. Edvard Brandes noted that "in his later years there lurked a strong sensuality in his bearing and speech."

Ibsen had, moreover, long regarded himself as a builder and his plays as works of architecture. In his youthful poem "Building Plans" he had compared the artist to a master builder; and when the painter Erik Werenskiold, seeing him looking at some new buildings in Christiania, asked: "You are interested in architecture?" Ibsen replied, "Yes; it is, as you know, my own trade." And Ibsen, like Solness, had always had a fear of looking down from a great height or into a chasm, and this had become worse as he had grown older.

It has been argued by several commentators that Solness's development as a builder corresponds precisely, if one reads between the lines, with Ibsen's career as a dramatist. "The churches which Solness sets out by building," suggested William Archer, "doubtless represent Ibsen's early romantic plays, the 'homes for human beings' his social dramas, while the houses with high towers, merging into 'castles in the air,' stand for those spiritual dramas, with a wide outlook over the metaphysical environment of humanity, on which he was henceforth to be engaged." The theory may at first seem fanciful, of the kind that Ibsen himself derided; but the more one ponders it, the more truthfully it rings, whether the analogy was conscious or not. And one interesting variant between his extant draft and the final version of the play reveals how closely he identified himself with Solness. In the second act, when Solness is telling Hilde how success came to him, Ibsen originally made him conclude with the words: "And now, at last, they have begun to talk of me abroad," which was exactly Ibsen's situation when he began work on the play. But he deleted the sentence in revision, doubtless because he felt that it made the identification too obvious.

Ibsen's interest in hypnosis, and the power that one human being could gain over the mind of another, has already been noted; and he carried it further in *The Master Builder* even than in his three preceding plays, concentrating here especially on how unexpressed wishes could sometimes translate themselves into actions. But if Solness is to be identified with Ibsen, Hilde is not to be identified with Emilie, Helene or Hildur. Was it from the needs of the play that Ibsen made her a harpy, or was it, remembering Elias's account of his maliciously untruthful description of Emilie, from a sense of guilt towards her and frustration with himself? Whatever the reason, from the time that Ibsen's letters to Emilie and Elias's story were published, both within a few months of Ibsen's death, everyone identified Emilie with Hilde, and for the remaining forty-eight years of her long life she was regarded as a predatory little monster.

—Michael Meyer, *Ibsen: A Biography* (Garden City, N.Y.: Doubleday, 1971): 696–698.

INGA-STINA EWBANK ON HOW PAST EVENTS SHAPE THE PLAY

[Inga-Stina Ewbank, Professor of German and Comparative Literature at the University of California–Davis, is author of *The Counterfeit Idyll* and *Women in Modern Drama*. In this passage, Ewbank discusses the way the characters reconstruct past events.]

Two moments in time past keep being re-activated in the process of reminiscences and reconstructions which makes up the text: the burning-down, some 'twelve-thirteen years ago', of Aline's family home, and Solness's climb, ten years since to the day, to the top of the tower he built for the church at Lysanger. In each case, what matters is not what 'really' happened, but how, and how differently, different characters perceive the significance of what happened. In each case, too, what is revealed at any given time depends on the nature of the interaction between speakers. When, on the subject of the fire, Solness and Aline in Act II drain each other with half-understood accusations, with self-explanations that are not wanted and with intended consolations that misfire, then words serve merely to alienate. Prompted by Hilde, on the other hand, each of them is able to reach down to the deepest sources of guilt and grief. With her, in Act III, Aline is drawn beyond the 'unbearable' sense of dereliction of duty to husband and newborn children which she tried to tell Solness about in Act II, to speak of the loss of the 'little things' that were her past and future: the family heirlooms and the nine dolls whom she 'carried under [her] heart. Like little unborn children.' And with Hilde, in Act II, Solness passionately lays bare his sense of responsibility for having *wished* the fire and the irrational guilt and fear of retribution which for ever undercut his achievement: 'That is the price my position as an artist has cost me—and others.'

Guilt slings to every version of the fire and drags people downwards. After hearing Aline's story, Hilde feels that she has been down a 'tomb', and earlier Solness speaks of his 'abysmal [literally, 'bottomless'], immeasurable debt' to Aline. Downward and upward forces clash in Solness's consciousness that, as he repeatedly says, the fire was what enabled him to rise ('*brakte meg i være*'). Hilde authenticates this sense of his calling as an upward trajectory, for which he has been singled out: 'Nobody but *you* should be allowed to build. You should do it all alone.' To see him 'standing free and high' on his own tower will affirm her faith in his power to do 'the impossible'.

The Lysanger episode alive in the play, not so much by gradual reconstruction as by Hilde imposing her construction of it on the Master Builder who, whether or not it is a fiction, is ever more willing to make it his own truth. If she is a '*dikter*', he begins as an ideal audience and ends up as a co-author, in a series of remarkable duologues where words and images are not only bridges but meeting points. By the end of Act I her account of events ten years ago has become 'something *experienced* [he] felt [he] had forgotten' (and it is a measure of the range of tones in their encounters that Hilde can teasingly praise him to Dr Herdal for this 'quite incredible memory'). In Act II her will-power is seen to empower him. Their dialogue begins like an illustration of Nietzsche's *Genealogy of Morals*, shot through with Solness's intense combination of self-castigation and self-affirmation. Knowing himself one of the 'specially chosen', his will implemented by mysterious 'helpers and servers', he is yet also living 'as if my chest was a great expanse of raw flesh' which never heals though 'these helpers and servers go flaying off skin from other people's bodies to patch my wound.' Hilde's unpitying response and accusation of 'a fragile conscience' mark a turning-point, with Solness, questioning the 'robustness' of Hilde's own conscience, beginning to take the lead in the dialogue. It is he who names as 'trolls' the motivating force about which she herself is inarticulate—'this thing inside me that drove and forced me here'—and who feeds her images of other reckless creatures—Vikings and birds of prey. Jointly, completing each other's sentences, they build their identification with these images, across a sub-text of sexual and spiritual affinity, charging every word with significance and creating a mythical world of their own. This Act closes with Hilde alone on stage, an image of Nietzschean 'reckless self-assurance', an a-moral will intent on a 'terribly exciting' repeat of Lysanger.

—Inga-Stina Ewbank, "The Last Plays." In *The Cambridge Companion to Ibsen*, ed. James McFarlane (Cambridge: Cambridge University Press, 1994): 141–143.

Plot Summary of
When We Dead Awaken

When We Dead Awaken was the last play Ibsen wrote, and it is also the shortest. Its theme is one that recurs throughout Ibsen's body of work: the price of greatness.

Rubek is a world famous sculptor who has returned to his native country (presumably Norway) after a long absence. He and his young, spirited wife go to a seaside health resort and there Rubek meets, after many years, Irene, the model for his greatest masterpiece, "Resurrection Day." Irene, who had once loved him, was not only his model but his inspiration. He was only interested in her as an artist, however, and she is still, after many years, shattered by this.

For the past few years, ever since he finished his masterpiece, he has worked only on portrait busts, but he tells his wife that underneath the "respectable faces" he sculpts are "stubborn muzzles of mules—lop-eared, low-browed dog skulls, and pampered pig snouts."

Rubek's wife, Maja, is a restless companion, ill-suited to Rubek's dark, brooding nature. At the spa she meets Ulfhejm, the bear hunter, who is stopping on his way to the mountains. Maja is taken with his wildness and she is eager to accompany him. Rubek has no objections.

When Rubek completed his masterpiece four or five years ago, he approached Irene and told her, "Thank you from the bottom of my heart, Irene. This . . . has been an extraordinary episode for me." Irene then realized that this was merely an episode for him and not an evolving, lifelong creation. Irene fled upon hearing that terrible word "episode," and they have both been living dead since that time.

Irene dredges up the past with Rubek, accusing him of using her soul and then discarding her. She has never recovered completely. Rubek listens patiently to all of her accusations: He realizes what he's done and that Irene is his only real salvation. Irene accuses Rubek, "Art first—and then human life." Rubek does not deny it. Rubek, like so many of Ibsen's heroes, has sacrificed human happiness in service of art. Rubek's great masterpiece, "Resurrection

Day," was created in Irene's image, but Irene perceives that when the work was finished, he was finished with her as well. He denies it, assuring her that he has created "No poetry since then. Just putterings in clay." And so she challenges him to rise again with her to the top of the mountain, to a new life which only she can give him, since her soul is also his. Irene asks him, "Do you have the courage to meet me one more time?"

He decides to leave his wife to climb to the top of the mountain with Irene, who is his true spiritual companion. As they climb, they rediscover each other. Maja is happy enough to be deserted, as she has attached herself to Ulfhejm, the bear hunter, who is much more her equal. The inevitable separation of Maja and Rubek is not lamented by anyone.

Rubek and Maja have been together for the four or five years since his separation from Irene, and Rubek has grown to realize that they are much too different to be happy together.

> MAJA: (looking sharply at him) Were you only interested in coaxing *me* out to play, too?
> RUBEK: (treating it as a joke) Well, hasn't it been a fairly amusing game?
> MAJA: (coolly) I didn't go off with you just to play games.
> RUBEK: No, no, certainly not.
> MAJA: And besides, you never took me up on any high mountains to show me—
> RUBEK: (irritably) All the glory of the world? No, I didn't. Because let me tell you something: you're really not made to climb mountains, Maja, my pet.

Only Irene is made to climb mountains and he will take her there, his true companion. To climb mountains is to rise in spirit, to enrich the self with things not of the earth. Just like his masterpiece was for him a "resurrection day," this reunion with Irene is also. When Rubek rejected Irene's love, he was rejecting life.

Irene is the idealized woman, inspiration incarnate. She perceives that her soul has been exploited since Rubek sculpted her and drew strength from her but refused to touch her, refused to truly love her. Yet only in union with Irene is he allowed any kind of peace. He cannot find the peace he is looking for in Maja, who is too much of the earth. Her best companion will be a hunter: Ulfhejm is her male counterpart. When she asks him what he hunts he replies,

"Bears by preference ma'am. But I don't mind taking on anything wild that comes my way. Eagles, wolves, women, elk, reindeer—so long as they're fresh and full-bodied, with plenty of blood in their veins." They prefer life as sport.

A storm sweeps through the mountain as Rubek and Irene climb higher and higher, while Maja and the bear hunter are descending to safety. Rubek and Irene awaken together after years of living death. There is an avalanche and Rubek and Irene are killed. Though they die in the end, we believe they are liberated, their souls free of the flesh in which Maja and the bear hunter revel.

The characters have gradually realigned in the play. Rubek goes up to the mountain top with Irene and Maja goes down to safety with her hunter. Maja declares that she is "putting life before anything else." Maja and Ulfhejm will accept life as it is while Rubek and Irene will be released from it altogether. Rubek and Irene ascend in pursuit of beauty and as they die they are followed by the words "*Pax vobiscum*," uttered by the nun. They are forgiven and given peace. Maja's words rise upward toward the couple lying dead in the avalanche:

> MAJA: I am free! I am free! I am free!
>   No more living in cages for me!
>   I am free as a bird! I am free!

As the four different characters discover each other, the setting of the play changes. It moves from the lawn of the health spa, to the woods near the resort, and finally to a fierce mountainside, "gashed with fissures." The terrain clearly symbolizes the spiritual eruption experienced by Rubek and Irene, if not also, on some level, by Maja and Ulfhejm. The event of their reunion becomes so ecstatic that it approaches the sublime. They are allowed then to transcend together through death. ❀

List of Characters in
When We Dead Awaken

Professor Arnold Rubek is a famous sculptor returning to his homeland (presumably Norway) after a long absence. His greatest single work is "Resurrection Day." The model for this piece was a woman named Irene who disappeared after the piece was complete. He has been restless and uninspired ever since.

Maja Rubek is Rubek's vivacious wife. She and Rubek are completely incompatible. She is an earthy woman, uninterested in art, and he finds her tedious. At the spa, she and Rubek eventually go their own ways. She meets a bear hunter who is much more suited to her than this man of art.

The **manager** of the spa is the man who introduces Maja to Ulfhejm, the bear hunter.

Ulfhejm is the bear hunter with whom Maja falls in love. He is the opposite of Rubek—he does not carefully sculpt an idealized woman but hunts and devours. He and Maja make a good pair and they descend down the mountain together.

Irene is a lady traveler the Rubeks encounter who once was Rubek's muse and the model for his most famous sculpture. When the sculpture was complete, she sensed that he had no more use for her, and so she fled. She has lived in a sort of spiritual void ever since, hating Rubek for discarding her.

A **nun** is Irene's attendant. She is a religious presence who hovers around Irene and Rubek as they find each other and ascend. ❀

Critical Views on
When We Dead Awaken

[Halvdan Koht, former minister of Norway, has written extensively on literary, social, and political subjects. Professor of History at the University of Oslo, he wrote of one of the standard biographies of Ibsen, *Life of Ibsen*, and co-edited a collection of Ibsen's works. Here Koht discusses Shakespeare's influence on Ibsen.]

Throughout his whole life, Ibsen was struggling to find and to express the fundamentals of his personality. That was the incessant fight within himself, his own personal drama. He was extremely sensitive to impressions from all of life and all the forces surrounding him, consequently from literature too. That sensitivity was an element of his genius, but he felt it also as a weakness. In his youth he was inclined to imitate all kinds of literary patterns, and even when out of the first flush of youth he might bow to the claims of ruling currents of thought. Such impressions might stimulate him to opposition, to efforts at creating something different, as when *Svend Dyring's House* by the Dane Henrik Hartz impelled him to show what the Norwegian folk-ballad, as contrasted with the Danish, might lead to in drama (*The Feast at Solhaug*, 1855). Or as, at a later date, *A Gauntlet* by Björnstjerne Björnson made him scorn the pretentious preachers of truth in *The Wild Duck*. Always he searched and fought for his own self.

Shakespeare helped him find himself. Shakespeare entered his life as a force of liberation. What he, vaguely and immaturely, strove to achieve in *Catiline*, now grew to be a mighty conscious effort, conforming with his very nature.

The Renaissance had taken hold of the ancient, classic literature in order to arm itself for the fight for intellectual freedom. When the young generations of Europe, from the 1770s on, rebelled against a fossilized, tyrannical classicism, they found in Shakespeare a powerful ally and fellow-fighter whom they could place in the vanguard of a new host of liberty. He remained the liberator even for later generations. We may compare his effect on Ibsen with that on Wergeland twenty-five years before. To Wergeland Shakespeare came at an earlier age and, from the start, overwhelmed him with such force as almost to drown his individuality. But soon he came to the surface again, refreshed and strengthened by the bath of passion and poetry; his poetic imagination had simply learned to find the rich expression corresponding to his innermost mind.

Ibsen was more mature when he met Shakespeare; he appropriated him more slowly, not with the violence of Wergeland, and he had no such period of complete Shakespearean imitation. Nevertheless, we can discern the first effects of Shakespeare in him by more material details than are visible in his later works.

—Halvdan Koht, "Shakespeare and Ibsen." In *Ibsen: A Collection of Critical Essays*, ed. Rolf Fjelde (Englewood Cliffs, N.J.: Prentice-Hall, 1965): 44–45.

LEO LOWENTHAL ON UNATTAINABLE HOPES

[Leo Lowenthal, Professor of Sociology at the University of California Berkeley, wrote *Literature, Popular Culture and Society*. In this essay, Lowenthal discusses the importance of personal relationships in Ibsen's plays.]

[Ibsen] does not write "social drama." Specific social, political or economic questions are touched upon only occasionally, as in *An Enemy of the People*, or *Pillars of Society*. Hardly ever does a policeman, soldier or other public official appear. The state seems to be reduced to the role of a night watchman. Official institutions appear only in such incidental business as the report of the prison sentence of old Borkman in *John Gabriel Borkman*, or as the threats of Dr. Wangel to call in the authorities against the Stranger in *The Lady from the Sea*. The scenes of Ibsen's plays are usually laid in the home, and the dialogue tends to be limited to the problems of the private person.

Here, however, we find the key to Ibsen's social concepts. He indicts society ⟨. . .⟩ in the sphere of private life where the individual can reveal himself freely. And this revelation shows man as the focal point for contradictions that originate in the society.

Public and private interests of the protagonists are portrayed as being inevitably irreconcilable. Energies available for use in public affairs deteriorate as soon as private needs and desires come into play. Solness, the Master Builder of churches and settlement houses, finds his only happiness in friendship with a young girl, whereupon he becomes completely lost in his dreams. The sculptor Rubek confesses to an emotional crisis when

> all the talk about the artist's vocation and the artist's mission and so forth began to strike me as being very empty, and hollow, and meaningless at bottom . . . Yes, is not life in sunshine and in beauty a hundred times better . . . ?

Allmers (in *Little Eyolf*) abandons his book, his great calling, to dedicate himself to the education of his son, little Eyolf, in order to "perfect all the rich possibilities that are dawning in his childish soul." These either-or attitudes are products of the isolation of the spheres of life. Not only does the pursuit of happiness in one realm require neglect of human obligations in every other, but even voluntary withdrawal from society cheats the individual of the happiness he seeks. The Master Builder never erects his dream castle but falls to his death from a real tower. The sculptor Rubek's (in *When We Dead Awaken*) original zest for life and art is lost in the tedium of a banal marriage. Eyolf's father is tortured by his unproductive existence, as well as by the jealousy of his wife and finally by the death of his child. Whether man turns to private or public life, as soon as he begins to develop his potentialities in one he runs into conflicts and frustrations in the other.

Ibsen's portrayals thus follow a pattern. A person starts out with the expectation of fulfillment. Then he finds himself involved in a series of conflicts and troubles which almost always bring ruin to him and force him to injure others. The result is solitude, death, or worse still, the announcement of social programs that have been thoroughly discredited by what has gone on before. Mankind is trapped in a cycle of unattainable hopes and real suffering.

Ibsen's dramas display a virtual catalogue of failure—in daily life, in the professions, in the arts, in marriage, in friendship, and in communication between the generations. Either the person cannot make an adjustment to these relationships, or he develops some of his powers at the expense of certain others or at the expense of his fellows. The discrepancy between the apparent wealth of potentialities and the narrow range of their fulfillment is a steadily recurrent motif.

—Leo Lowenthal, "Henrik Ibsen: Motifs in the Realistic Plays." In *Ibsen: A Collection of Critical Essays*, ed. Rolf Fjelde (Englewood Cliffs, N.J.: Prentice-Hall, 1965): 140–141.

F. W. KAUFMANN ON THE SEARCH FOR TRUTH

[F. W. Kaufmann, chairman of the Department of German and Russian at Oberlin College, has published studies of Schiller and German dramatists of the nineteenth century. In this excerpt, Kaufmann discusses Ibsen's pursuit of truth.]

If any proof were needed that Ibsen's fight for emancipation from traditional moral demands and the pressure of social norms is not to be confused with moral anarchy, but rather a challenge to assume more personal responsibility, one may refer to two plays, one written at the beginning and the other at the end of his modern period. While Brand believed it possible to acquire the absolute truth, Peer Gynt represents a moral relativism in the extreme where it approaches nihilism. He rushes from one experience [to another], never exhausting the potentialities of any and never involving himself enough to experience the truth behind the transitory phenomenon. His world is a world of mere facts and incidents, because he is incapable of giving his experiences any relevant truth by a serious effort to integrate them through personal involvement. Because he cannot be true to himself, his life is one continuous series of deceptions and self-deceptions. The truth he should have lived is symbolized in Solveig, whose dramatic function corresponds to the *Deus Caritatis* in *Brand*. Solveig is the symbol of the self-transcending orientation towards that integral oneness which alone is truth.

Peer Gynt may be considered a nineteenth-century caricature of Faust who deludes himself into the belief that his superficial and aimless activities will contribute to his self-realization, the fool of a morality play in a modernized version. Hedda Gabler, on the other hand, is a sophisticated woman who has been neglected and never been understood in her youth, and who takes revenge for her frustrated emotional life by stimulating the emotions of a man like Lövborg to an orgiastic pitch and then dismissing him in favor of the most philistine pedant for whom she cannot feel anything but contempt. A sophisticated lady who admits to herself that she has no talent for anything but boredom, she hates all norms as hypocritical while at the same time she poisons the lives of everyone, including herself, by her absolute disregard of the truth in all her personal relations. ⟨. . .⟩

Ibsen's last dramas may bear final witness to the fact that for him truth was not a social issue, but an eminently vital personal concern. In *The Master Builder* Solness torments himself with the question of whether he dedicated his whole art to the service of truth, or whether he betrayed that ideal by making concessions to the everyday needs of society; whether he expressed himself and his ideals in his creations or whether he tried to satisfy the masses with sham values. In *When We Dead Awaken* the artist Rubek confesses that he failed in his obligation to actualize the ideal in his life, and instead turned to the creation of monsters, or, if we interpret the symbol as Ibsen's self-confession, he first tried to find the truth in the abstract realm of the ideal demand and then lost himself in the portrayal of characters who were either satisfied in living their "life's lies" or vainly struggling for freedom in truth. The self-criticism of these last plays, however, illustrates again that Ibsen's conception of truth is as distant from abstract demands as it is from the chaotic concreteness of life.

In summary we may state that Ibsen's conception of truth is far more encompassing than what is ordinarily meant by the term; even the substitution of the term truthfulness is not sufficient to describe the whole complex of the problem. Although Ibsen's plays seem to be mainly concerned with the opposite of truth, the "life's lie," the ideal of truth is never quite absent; it is represented in the struggle of characters who even in their failure and because of their very failure point in the direction of that truth which, as the letters show, is for Ibsen the creative response to life, originating in concrete situations and transcending them without vanishing in the lifeless realm of the abstract.

—F. W. Kaufmann, "Ibsen's Conception of Truth." In *Ibsen: A Collection of Critical Essays*, ed. Rolf Fjelde (Englewood Cliffs, N.J.: Prentice-Hall, 1965): 26–28.

RICHARD SCHECHNER ON RUBEK'S VISION

[Richard Schechner is a writer and director. He is the author of a book on Eugene Ionesco and the editor of the *Tulane Drama Review*. Here Schechner discusses the role of the artist in Ibsen.]

When We Dead Awaken comes closest to giving us Ibsen's definitive statement on the artist and therefore demands, in this regard, special attention. Irene ⟨. . .⟩ continually emphasizes two things: her nakedness and her murders. And her great outcry against Rubek is forthrightly stated:

> I stripped myself naked for you to gaze at me. (*More quietly*) And you never once touched me.

This is the heart-piercing rage of humanity against the artist. For Irene here represents the human soul which is laid bare by the artist and she despairingly resents the fact that the artist does not love, but like God himself, ascetically creates. In these lines are the mysteries of art, which takes to itself, uses all that is most human but which cannot itself enter into the quintessential human condition: love. Rubek answers Irene's cry:

> Irene, didn't you understand that your beauty often drove me almost out of my mind? . . . [But] before all else, I was an artist. And I was sick—sick with a longing to create the one great work of my life.

And since Irene is the personified thought of Rubek himself, his cry is against life itself which is beautiful and drives the artist near out of his mind for longing, but which he cannot touch. It is the work—the creation of the artist—which is his "child," as Rubek notes: the hard, self-formed, immortal art-work. The relationship between Rubek and his sculpture is the only love relationship there can be for him. And this love is, at best, metaphorical. When man becomes God he surrenders his humanity—Irene—continually haunts him and finally comes to take what it owns in the final act of his life.

I mentioned before that the havoc which the artist creates within himself inflicts itself upon those who love him. It is this havoc which is symbolized by Irene's murders. We are not asked to believe that she actually killed others. Rubek has killed the soul in her and therefore anyone who loves her is damaged in turn. The disease of art, although neutralized in the art-work, passes on from person to person. The "fine, sharp dagger" which Irene always takes to bed with her and with which she almost kills Rubek is the psychical memento of Rubek's art: the death of love, of the soul.

In *The Master Builder, John Gabriel Borkman,* and *When We Dead Awaken* the artist is in contention with himself, with his vision. What Ibsen saw, and reflected dramatically, is the titanic isolation of the artist: alone with himself and those ideas which mirror him. The artist recognizes this isolation and deplores it. He shuns his daemonic ideas and tries to give up art for the sake of humanity. He vows to build homes for human beings, to do striking likenesses which are at heart nice domestic animals, or to wait for the world to call him to practical leadership.

But, finally, the artist realizes that this lower road is not for him. He returns to the mountain of his vision—the tower of his super-human aspiration where he must face in all its nakedness the pure power and beauty of the clear, cold transcendental truth. It is not by accident that these three plays all end in high, cold, and lonely places. Jung suggests that "the mountain stands for the goal of the pilgrimage and ascent, hence it often has the psychological meaning of the self." And, indeed, it is on high that Solness, Borkman, and Rubek all ultimately face what they are: artists. Prodded by his daemonic ego, atop his peak, the artist catches a last glimpse of the immutable and ineffable. Realizing that it is just so—he sees, knows, and dies. Below him, the institutions of man with their righteous strait-jackets and their codes that work utter a forgiving and perhaps worshipping *Pax Vobiscum!* Those who cannot understand—the great mass of individual human beings—sing on merrily that they are free—"from further down the mountainside."

—Richard Schechner, "The Unexpected Visitor in Ibsen's Late Plays." In *Ibsen: A Collection of Critical Essays*, ed. Rolf Fjelde (Englewood Cliffs, N.J.: Prentice-Hall, 1965): 163–164.

SIMON WILLIAMS ON IBSEN'S LEGACY

[Simon Williams, Professor of Dramatic Art at the University of California–Santa Barbara has published *German Actors of the Eighteenth and Nineteenth Centuries* and *Shakespeare on the German Stage*. In this extract, Williams discusses Ibsen's effect on theater.]

There were, of course, striking innovations in Ibsen's drama, but in retrospect they appear more as evolutionary developments than radical breaks with past practice. Although conservative critics deplored the vast amount of time devoted to exposition, the more discerning welcomed the greater structural cohesion this gave the action, finding exposition to invest the realistic drama with unwonted classical proportions and to intensify the tragic perspective on a mundane world. Attention to exposition and the self-exploration this required of major characters meant that an Ibsen play struck contemporaries as, in Henry James's words, 'the picture not of an action but of a condition . . . of a state of nerves as well as of soul, a state of temper, of health, of chagrin, of despair'. The consequence of this focus on character was an apparent de-theatricalization; in fact to the admirer of Ibsen, the word 'theatrical' had negative connotations, implying whatever was 'inauthentic'. Looked at historically, it is clear that through Ibsen the conventions of an earlier generation were beginning to lose their credibility. The plays and their performers were constantly praised for their denial of theatricality and their capacity to create a strikingly convincing illusion of everyday life. 'The effect of the play,' Ibsen wrote about *Ghosts*, 'depends a great deal on making the spectator feel as if he were actually sitting, listening, and looking at events happening in real life.' However unsettling their impact was upon the audience, aesthetically his works remained within the range of conventional thinking about theatre.

Two further qualities of Ibsen's work made it historically important. First, as he was concerned not with ideal models of behaviour but with revealing motives that lie beneath the surface of behaviour, Ibsen's plays were not especially pleasant. While George Bernard Shaw's claim—that attending an Ibsen play was like the fascinating but painful experience of going to the dentist—should be taken for the rhetoric it is, it indicates a new dimension to theatregoing. The play was no longer staged solely for entertainment, and the actors needed no longer to ingratiate themselves with the audience. A novel and potentially antagonistic relationship was thereby set up between stage and auditorium, an antagonism that was a prime stimulus for the initial critical outcry. Secondly, as characters became complex and revealed their personalities through the non-linear medium of memory and as much of this revelation centered around symbols that were difficult to grasp, Ibsen seemed to be asking for more imaginative effort from his audience than any playwright prior to him had done. He was not easy to follow, though as the French critic Jules Lemaitre put it when discussing *Hedda Gabler,* sometimes it is necessary in the theatre 'to reflect, to make an effort, to work'.

—Simon Williams, "Ibsen and the Theatre 1877–1900." In *The Cambridge Companion to Ibsen*, ed. James McFarlane (Cambridge: Cambridge University Press, 1994): 171–172.

Plot Summary of
Peer Gynt

Peer Gynt, based very loosely on a character from Norwegian folk-lore, is the story of a shiftless compromiser, a braggart, and most significantly, a man who will do anything to maintain his own illusions about himself. It is important to know that, in telling this tale, Ibsen does not restrict himself to reality, but constructs elaborate passages of fantasy, and it is often difficult to tell where reality ends and Peer's dreams begin. Peer's hallucinations are sometimes obvious to the reader as such, but not always. Removing the story even further from reality, the play is composed complete in rhymed verse. This is the last play Ibsen would write in verse form. It is five acts long, and it was written with no thought of performance—only for the reader—though it has been performed. In fact, it was not called a drama but a dramatic poem.

As the play opens, Peer's mother, Aase, is scolding him for tearing his clothes, for being lazy and for lying. Though this seems the interaction of a mother and young boy, Peer is about twenty. Aase is fed up with his inventions and alleged adventures. She laments that she has a disgrace of a son but Peer assures her that he was born to die a "nobler death" and the two of them go off to the wedding at Hegstad Farm. Uninvited, Peer is disdained by all the guests but one, Solveig, who falls madly in love with him. Peer, in a moment of complete audacity, decides to steal the bride and spirits her off to the mountainside where she then leaves him.

Here the play shifts into fantasy. Peer encounters the troll people deep in the woods. He tells the Woman in Green that he is a prince. She tells him that she is a princess and takes him to an entire kingdom of trolls, ruled by the Troll King, her father. Peer offers her his little hut as a palace. The Troll King and his court are pleased that Peer is willing to reject his Christian life and they entreat him to have his eyes maimed, so that he will be cured of his human nature and become pure troll. The sacrifice of his eyes would allow him to see things as he wishes to see them rather than how they are. But he refuses and flees.

In the grips of the darkness, he hears a voice. Peer asks who he is and the voice replies "Myself, can you say the same?" This question will become like a refrain throughout the play. Is Peer himself? What does it mean to be oneself? When Peer asks the voice again to identify himself, he tells Peer that he is the Great Boyg and encourages him to take a "roundabout" path. The Great Boyg is encouraging him to avoid facing the truth.

Peer goes deeper still into the woods and a builds his own little hut. Solveig finds him there and wants to make a home with him. She devotes herself to him, but he leaves anyway, telling her to wait for him.

Peer travels far and wide and we meet him again on the southwest coast of Morocco where he is telling some fellow travelers about his adventures, and how he prospered in America as a slave-trader, whisky peddler, and the like. Now he is rich—fate has provided well for him. He tells them he plans to be an emperor. They then proceed to steal his ship, crew, and fortune. He is shaken until he sees them blow-up when the steam ship explodes, and he knows once again that God is on his side.

He then finds a white horse in the desert and is met by an Arabian tribe who believes him to be the Messiah. He feels that he is now truly himself because he is respected for who he is rather than for his money. He falls in love with one of the dancing girls who makes off with his horse and leaves him again alone in the desert.

He wanders to the Great Sphinx where he encounters a German man trying to comprehend the Sphinx. Peer tells the man that the Sphinx is itself and the man decides Peer must be a genius. He invites Peer back to a club of learned men in Cairo. Peer accompanies him, and the club turns out to be a madhouse in which the inmates have escaped and have taken their keepers hostage. It is in the madhouse that Peer is crowned Emperor of Himself. He is being glorified as he collapses in confusion and exhaustion.

We meet Peer again as an old man returning to the scenes of his early adventures. Finally he meets a button molder who wants his soul to melt down with other souls. The button molder is sad that Peer never was himself and will use the scrap of Peer's soul to create something new and better. But Peer breaks free of this moment of death, not once but three times, each time the button molder asks

Peer to give him some proof that he was himself. But Peer cannot even be sure he understands what it is to be himself. Peer cannot prove that he was anything at all, not even an adequate sinner. He is worthy neither of heaven nor of hell.

In his third escape he encounters Solveig, now an old woman, who has waited for him all these years. He begs her to hide him. She forgives him of everything. And the button molder whispers a reminder to Peer about their next meeting.

Directly before *Peer Gynt*, Ibsen wrote the play *Brand*, the story of a ruthless religious zealot who made absolute pronouncements, forced sacrifices on himself, his family and congregation, and eventually is destroyed by the his own rigorous ideals. "Ibsen's mind must have played with the possibility of creating his counterpart, the man with no ruling passion, no calling, no commitment, the eternal opportunist, the mirror of surfaces, the charming, gifted, self-centered child who turns out finally to have neither center nor self," writes Ibsen scholar Rolf Fjelde.

Ibsen wanted to create a hollow man, who searches half-heartedly for his own identity, refusing to see the world honestly, a man who cannot carry through with any action for fear of finding his true self at the end. Peer Gynt is representative of a great many of Ibsen's fears and antipathies, including demons within himself.

Right before Ibsen wrote *Peer Gynt*, he had been deeply angered by the Norwegian response to the Dano-Prussian War. In December of 1863, the Prussians invaded Denmark, and the Norwegians, having committed to action in the face of external aggression to any of the Scandinavian countries (Norway, Denmark, Sweden) remained neutral. On one level, Ibsen wanted to draw a portrait of a people who made boasts and promises but were ultimately impotent. To embody this idea, Ibsen chose a character from Norwegian folklore, Peer Gynt, who was an idealized peasant hero, and he twisted him into a mock version of the original. Georg Brandes, a contemporary of Ibsen's, reviewed the bitter play, saying, "Contempt for humanity and self-hatred make a bad foundation on which to build a poetic work."

This scathing, satirical play was not merely an indictment, however. It was an exploration of the unconscious. In particular, the

Voice in the Darkness, who identifies himself to Peer as the Great Boyg, is Peer's subconscious mandating that he "go roundabout." This is what the Great Boyg tells him to do and this is how, for the rest of his life he acts in the face of decision. The Great Boyg is a symbolic presence that has been interpreted many ways. In Norwegian folklore it has been described as an invisible gigantic beast resembling a snake or an enormous, invisible troll. It has been translated "the great Between." The word *boyg* is related to the German *beugen,* which means to curve, meander, or bend. It is generally accepted that whatever the Great Boyg represents, it emanates from the depths of Peer's own self. It is his lack of will, or those things which prevent him from becoming himself.

When we are introduced to Peer Gynt, he is described as a powerfully built youth of twenty. He tells his mother a tale about riding on the back of a reindeer. The image of Peer riding the wild animal is man and nature as one, unreflective, brutish, childish or in Ibsen's universe, trollish. Again we have the concept of the troll in *Peer Gynt.* Never is Ibsen more literal about the trolls than he is in this play. While we are not necessarily expected to believe we are experiencing anything but Peer's imagination, Ibsen himself gives the creatures no other name than Trolls.

According to Francis Bull, trolls are "the evil forces of Nature . . . embodying and symbolizing those powers of evil, hidden in the soul of man, which may at times suppress his conscious will and dominate his actions." M. C. Bradbook described the troll as "the animal version of man, the alternative to man; he is also what man fears he may become."

Peer has always suffered from his own delusions, but when he steals the bride, Ingrid, away into the mountainside, we are drawn into his illusions with him. The troll scenes are again, a projection of Peer's unconscious, and yet they are also a gruesome recapitulation of the previous scene—the proper wedding. The wedding guests are merely better concealers of their inner-trolls. They are the bourgeois whom Ibsen wants to expose as an orgy of trolls. (To completely understand the wildness of the scene in the Royal Hall of the Troll King it is important to know that much of the basic material was freely adapted from Hans Christian Andersen's tale "Elf Hill." Andersen, the famous children's writer, was writing at the same time as Ibsen; he knew Ibsen, and read his work as well.)

In **Act 2, Scene 6,** the Troll King asks Peer what the difference is between troll and man and Peer replies there is none at all. The Troll King agrees except for one difference:

> TROLL KING: Outside
> Among men, under the shining sky,
> They say: "Man, to yourself be true!"
> While here, under our mountain roof,
> We say: "Troll, to yourself be—enough!"

Men strive to realize themselves but trolls are sufficient in whomever they are. They are complete. Peer is even unable to commit to the troll's simple directive, so he flees the troll kingdom in search of himself. When he escapes, he encounters the Great Boyg. Peer hears the voice in the woods and asks him who he is. "Myself" replies the voice, "can you say the same?" From this point Peer will strive to become himself. Unsure even what he is working towards, he will proclaim over and over, that he has finally become himself, Emperor Peer Gynt.

The whole action of the play is directed toward Peer making this discovery. To become man is the goal, to leave the troll behind and realize the self. But what is it to become a man? Ibsen gives us a self-realized man who lives quietly in the background of the play. It is the farm boy who, in **Act Three**, amputates his finger to avoid being drafted into the war, and in Act Five, fifty years later, is buried as a Pastor gives his eulogy. Though the farm boy committed a cowardly act, he was redeemed by living his life honestly, through droughts and fires, through hunger and pain. He raised his children and worked his land and consequently became himself.

The Pastor recalls him in **Act Five**:

> There he was great, because he was himself.
> His inborn note was steadfast as a star.
> His life was music, like a muted bell.
> So, peace be with you, silent warrior,
> Who fought the peasant's little fight, and fell.
> It's not our place to sift the heart and soul—
> That's not for dust, but for the Judge of all—
> Still I believe—and here it must be said:
> This man stands now no cripple to his God!

After Peer's encounter in the forest with the Great Boyg, he descends deeper still into the mountainside and builds a hut, where

Solveig, the young woman he met at the wedding, comes and is ready to devote herself to him. Solveig is everything that the trolls are not. She stakes all her life on one decision: to wait for Peer. She is the final cause of hope for Peer's soul in the play. But Peer avoids her devotedness, he runs off and tells her to wait. She does wait—fifty years.

Peer sets out to America where he makes his fortune doing all variety of disreputable things, even slave trading. He then takes his riches to Africa where he intends to make himself an emperor. His first attempt is foiled, and then entirely by chance, a tribe of Arabs encounters him on a white horse and declares him the messiah. But he is soon dethroned again when a dancing girl makes off with his horse. Peer is alone in the desert, alone with himself, unsure who he is.

In **Act Four,** he encounters the Sphinx, and we recall Oedipus who confronted him and was able to surmount him by answering the riddle. But Peer does not answer a riddle because he is not even quiet long enough to listen. He asks questions of the Sphinx to which the Sphinx is mute. A man sits trying to comprehend the great monument when Peer declares that the Sphinx is itself and the man rejoices in this profound answer. He takes Peer back to his club in Cairo which turns out to be a madhouse. Only here, at the end of Peer's life, gripped with terror and surrounded by insanity, is he finally declared by the inmates, Emperor of Himself. At the end of Act Four he collapses in the madhouse. Finally comes the moment of death extended over the entirety of Act Five.

In Act Five, Peer meets the Button Molder who, as God's emissary, is ready to take Peer's soul and melt it down with a host of others. Peer begs for another chance at life, and the Button Molder asks Peer to give him some proof that he was himself. Peer must eventually confess on his third meeting with the Button Molder that he does not know what it means to become oneself. The Button Molder tells Peer that one must first lose the self. To be yourself is to slay yourself. This idea has overtones of Matthew 16: 25–26, but more directly concerns the choice first stated by the Troll King, namely, to kill one's self-sufficiency in order to become the open, full self.

At the end of the play, the sun rises as Solveig holds Peer in her arms. He pleads with her desperately to "hide me within."

This concept is directly from John 3:3–7. The sunrise may be an allusion to the folktales in which sunrise vanquishes the troll monster, but again it is also biblical. The first rays of light on world are things beginning again, and Peer can be hopeful at last.

Peer is taking Solveig as more than just as his savior. Solveig is hope, death, and mother in one. The play ends:

> SOLVEIG: Sleep in my arms; I'll watch over thee—
> Sleep and dream, my dearest boy!

In *Peer Gynt*, Ibsen was writing about himself no more or less than in his other plays. Ibsen once wrote: "To live is to war with trolls in heart and soul. To write is to sit in judgment on oneself." As always he dramatized his inner struggle including a terrible fear of the potentialities of himself. ❀

List of Characters in
Peer Gynt

Aase is a farmer's widow and Peer's mother.

Peer Gynt, her son, is a powerfully built youth of twenty and the embodiment of unrealized man. He is like a child, and his fantastic adventures hopefully lead him to himself.

Ingrid's **wedding guests** are not receptive of Peer, knowing his reputation.

A **newcomer and his wife** are the parents of Solveig and little Helga. **Solveig** is the woman who waits a lifetime for Peer, who redeems him in the end, and little **Helga** is the sister she looks after.

The **farmer** at Hegstad is the father of **Ingrid,** who is about to be married when Peer carries her off. She does not want to be married and is thus receptive to Peer's advances.

Three herd girls from a mountain hut mark the beginning of Peer's descent in the troll world.

A **woman in green** is the troll girl Peer is willing to take as his princess until her father, the Troll King, demands that he slit his eyes. He has a child with her, who is called **an ugly brat.**

The **Troll King** is the father of the woman in green and the man who hopes to initiate Peer into the world of trolls. He is not successful.

Kari is a cottar's wife.

A **voice in the darkness** and **bird cries** haunt Peer as he escapes the Troll kingdom. The voice in the darkness identifies himself as the **Great Boyg.**

Mr. Cotton, Mr. Ballon, Herr von Eberkopf and **Herr Trumpeterstraale,** a **thief,** and a **fence,** all traveling gentlemen, are the men to whom Peer boasts about his adventures in America. Then they make off with his ship and his fortune.

The **Statue of Memnon** (singing) and the **Sphinx at Gizeh** (mute) are the two monuments Peer comes to in the desert, trying to discover some morsel of wisdom from them. At the Sphinx he encounters **Professor Begriffenfeldt,** director of the insane asylum at Cairo.

Peer encounters **Huhu,** a language reformer from the Malabar coast, a **Fellah** with a royal mummy and **Hussein**, a Near Eastern cabinet minister, and other **inmates**, along with their **keepers** when Professor Begriffenfeldt takes Peer to his club in Cairo for learned men. The club turns out to be an insane asylum from which the lunatics have escaped and hold their keepers hostage.

Peer encounters a **Norwegian sea captain**, his crew, and a **strange passenger** on his voyage back over all the events of his life.

In the final passage to enlightenment, Peer passes by the funeral of the **farm boy** and hears the eulogy given. He still doesn't understand that the farm boy was the exemplar of a man who found himself.

The **Button Molder** is an emissary from God who has come to take Peer's soul and melt it down with others in order to create a new and better one. Peer's soul is not meant for heaven, but it is not even soiled enough for hell. The **lean person** is an Emissary from Satan who does not deem Peer enough of a sinner. And so Peer must be melted down. ✦

Critical Views on
Peer Gynt

GEORG GRODDECK ON THE PSYCHOLOGY OF THE PLAY

[Georg Groddeck (1866–1934) was a German psychothera-
pist and a pioneer in the field of psychosomatic medicine.
Among his books are *The Book of the It, The World of Man,*
and *The Unknown Self.* In this excerpt, he discusses Peer
Gynt's inability to change and his satisfaction with the self
he already is.]

Peer Gynt is just as all other men are—that is true even though
not every man can see the truth—only unfortunately many of us
try to seem different. He is really himself, he does not need to
grow on himself. He is a dreamer, but he knows quite well that
he dreams and fantasies. Other people call him a liar—the first
words in the play are those of his mother: "You are lying"—the
prince of liars, but that is sheer stupidity on their part, for he is
essentially sincere. By nature man is forced to daydream, to build
his fantasies, but his fancy must be self-sufficient; the man who
wants to turn fantasy into reality, or who thinks for a moment
that this is possible, that man is the liar, for he does not remain
true to himself. Peer never cherishes this vain intention, but
keeps fantasy and reality clearly apart; his fantasies represent no
aim in life for him, he merely lives in them and has no other use
for them. He remains himself when he is daydreaming just as he
does when he eats or drinks or peels his onion. Never does he lose
hold of himself in his dreams, never does he make the usual
feeble compromise of transferring some small part of dream life
into the world of every day. He is always Emperor Peer Gynt.
Certainly he does little for the state or the well-being of his fellow-
countrymen; the words spoken by the pastor at a burial apply
equally to him:

> A breaker of the law? Perhaps—
> Yet something shines above all laws,
> Even as the crown of mist
> Above the mountain-top.
> A worthless citizen, who served
> No king or country?

> Yet was he great because he was himself,
> Because he never stilled the voice within,
> That voice which sighed like muted violin.

Peer himself adopts this verdict as his own epitaph:

> A time will come when yonder worthy man
> Shall say the same of me.

And now that time has come, for Ibsen's readers are inspired by Peer's vitality, some of them without understanding why, and some even completely mistaking what it is in him that makes him so sympathetic a character. Many of those who read or see the play imagine that Solveig is the salvation of a ruined and depraved Peer, but Solveig is not very different. She, too, is herself, only she knows nothing about it, can know nothing. ⟨. . .⟩ For the Philistine—and it is very hard to come out of Philistia—Peer Gynt wastes his life in trifles, dabbles in wickedness without ever committing an honest crime, and is not even worth sending to hell but must be melted down in the Button-molder's spoon. Is Solveig, though, any whit better? Does she not also waste her life by sitting in the mountains and waiting for a man with whom she has only spoken three times, whom everybody calls a liar—and judged by their standards he deserves the name—who is the son of a drunken father and a crazy mother, who holds nothing sacred, but rushes about the world, is slave-owner and false prophet, who falls into the power of trolls, and snaps his fingers at the devil? Has Solveig nothing better to do than mind a few goats? Is she to be forgiven for deserting her worthy parents, and throwing herself at the head of a stranger, a notorious swindler? Does she not dabble in wickedness also, or is she supposed to be better because the word "fidelity" governs her life? To whom, then, is she faithful? Only to herself. Not to Peer Gynt, for she does not know him. To herself. Just as he remains himself, so also does she, only she is a woman and he a man.

—Georg Groddeck, "Peer Gynt." In *Ibsen: A Collection of Critical Essays*, ed. Rolf Fjelde (Englewood Cliffs, N.J.: Prentice-Hall, 1965): 69–70.

[John Northam, Fellow of Clare College, sometimes University Lecturer in English, Cambridge University, and Emeritus Professor of Modern and Comparative Drama, University of Bristol lists *Ibsen's Dramatic Method: A Study of the Prose Dramas, Ibsen: A Critical Study* and *Ibsen's Poems*, among his publications. In this extract, Northam discusses Ibsen's tragic hero.]

"What is the modern tragic conflict; or, where is the tragic hero to be found in modern life?" This seems to me a pertinent question to ask about the literature of the last hundred odd years and particularly of the last decade. It is pertinent not merely because ordinary people nowadays are not very heroic in their daily lives—I doubt if they have ever been that—but because our own generation is so peculiarly deficient even in the *idea* of a hero. Unlike the Greeks and the Elizabethans, we have no definite and exalted place reserved in our scheme of things for the hero. The most prevalent fashion in our literature is to explore, sometimes with a wry humor, the suffering and the defeat, the pathos of human existence, or to express anger; but rarely does it offer any more invigorating example.

It is because tragedy is so invigorating, besides being dreadful and terrifying, that it is vital to the spiritual health of an age. It suggests to us standards by which, even in the commonplace society which we inhabit, life can become an expression of nobility. That is why Ibsen is so vitally important to us, for he seems to me to be the only dramatist to have created great tragedy out of a society that can still be called fundamentally modern.

Tragedy has resisted definition long enough for it to be in no danger from me; but it will help the argument if I indicate crudely and briefly what I understand by the term. Tragedy explores the extent to which man is responsible for his own fate. Exploration is needed, because although man acts on the assumption that he is free to choose, he comes into conflict with powers in the universe over which he has no ultimate control. There is no fixed or clear demarcation between freedom and necessity.

Whether, in any particular play, man will be portrayed primarily as an individual or as a figure representative of mankind as a whole seems to depend on the attitudes current in the community out of which the play is created. It is not surprising that in the prime of the Athenian city state, a tightly organized society, the tragic heroes of Aeschylus were presented not as individuals but as great symbols of mankind. It is the cross-fertilization of medieval and Renaissance ideas that enables Shakespeare to present figures that are simultaneously great typical figures and also individuals observed with miraculous attention to detail.

For Ibsen, coming when he did in time, there could be no question but that the hero must be represented primarily as an individual. So that one of the problems facing Ibsen, if we can credit him with a constant ambition to write a modern tragedy, was this: how to present on the stage a convincing portrait of a modern individual— a man of sophisticated and subtle thoughts and feelings. of modern manners and of everyday speech—and at the same time show him as possessing the full stature and grandeur of a hero.

—John Northam, "Ibsen's Search for the Hero." In *Ibsen: A Collection of Critical Essays*, ed. Rolf Fjelde (Englewood Cliffs, N.J.: Prentice-Hall, 1965): 91–92.

MARTIN ESSLIN ON IBSEN'S POETIC STYLE

[Martin Esslin fled Vienna in 1938 where he was studying to become a director, to escape the Nazi invasion of Austria. He became a British citizen and worked as writer and drama critic for the BBC. His most influential book, *The Theater of the Absurd*, came out in 1961. Other works include *Reflections: Essays on Modern Theatre, The Peopled Wound: The Work of Harold Pinter*, and a collection of his radio talks, *An Anatomy of Drama*. In this excerpt, Esslin discusses the poetic quality of Ibsen's work.]

⟨T⟩he action shifts from the external world into the protagonists' dreams or fantasies: ⟨. . .⟩ the Troll scenes in *Peer Gynt*, Peer Gynt's shipwreck, the whole Button Moulder sequence and, indeed, the final vision of Solveig, are dreamlike projections of the characters' inner visions. When Ibsen made the decision to devote himself to realistic prose drama these dream and fantasy elements were—on the surface—suppressed. Yet they are continuously present, nevertheless. They emerge above all in what has come to be regarded as Ibsen's increasing resort to symbolism. Having renounced the use of *poetry in the theatre* (in the form of verse or grandly poetic subject matter) Ibsen made more and more use of *poetry of the theatre* which emerges from the sudden transformation of a real object into a symbol, from the metaphoric power of an entrance or an exit, a door opening or closing, a glance, a raised eyebrow or a flickering candle.

It is my contention—and conviction—that the continuing power and impact of Ibsen's plays spring from precisely this poetic quality. If we accept that all fiction, however realistic its form, is ultimately the product of the imagination, the fantasy-life, the daydreaming of its author, then even the most realistic drama call be seen, ultimately, as a fantasy, a daydream. The more creative, the more complex, the more original, the more poetic the imagination of the writer, the greater will be this element in his work. It is one of the hallmarks of the best work of some of our foremost contemporary playwrights that they are conscious of this position and make use of it. The plays of Edward Bond and Harold Pinter, to name but those who most readily come to mind, are examples of this tendency: they are conceived as working both on the level of extreme realism and at the same time on that of fantasy and dream. In this they have surely been anticipated by Ibsen. The continued and undiminished impact of even Ibsen's most seemingly political plays owes, in my opinion, a great deal to that immense hidden and mysterious power which springs from the co-existence of the realistic surface with the deep subconscious fantasy and dream elements behind it: the simulated forest wilderness in the attic of *The Wild Duck*, the white horses of *Rosmersholm*, the ghosts that haunt Mrs. Alving, the mysterious Stranger of *The Lady from the Sea*, the spectral Rat Wife of *Little Eyolf*, Borkman's self-created prison, Løvborg's manuscript as Hedda's aborted dream-child, the haunting appearance of the destructive and seductive Hilda Wangel in *The Master Builder*, Aline's dolls in the same place—they all are powerful poetic metaphors, fantasy-images as well as real objects and forces which can be perceived in a sober, factual light.

For, ultimately, the power of all drama springs from its innermost poetic nature as a metaphor of reality, a representation of the whole of reality which of necessity must include the internal world, the world of the mind (both conscious and subconscious), as well as the external reality of rooms, furniture, and cups of coffee. As soon as that external reality is put on the stage it becomes, by the very nature of the theatrical phenomenon, an image, a metaphor of itself: *imaged,* imagined, and by that very fact a mental, a fantasy phenomenon. '*Alles Vergaengliche ist nur ein Gleichnis*', as Goethe puts it in the final scene of *Faust:* all our ephemeral, evanescent reality is itself, ultimately, merely metaphor, symbol.

It is this quality of the metaphorical power, the poetic vision behind the realistic surface of Ibsen's later plays—their impact as images, and the complex allusive representations of those aspects of human existence, those problems that lie beyond the expressive resources of merely discursive language—in which their real greatness and enduring impact lies. And these, precisely, are the elements in Ibsen which are both highly traditional as well as continuously contemporary, continuously modern.

> —Martin Esslin, "Ibsen and Modern Drama." In *Ibsen and the Theatre: The Dramatist in Production*, ed. Erroll Durbach (New York: New York University Press, 1980): 81–82.

JAMES MCFARLANE ON SOURCES FOR THE PLAY

[James McFarlane is Emeritus Professor of European Literature at the University of East Anglia. He was General Editor of the eight-volume *Oxford Ibsen* and is the author of several books on Ibsen and other literary topics, including *Ibsen and Meaning.* Here McFarlane discusses a source of *Peer Gynt* and the fantasy aspects of the play.]

Literary scholarship has been assiduous in tracing a whole series of sources—in legend, myth, folk-tale, works of literature, as well as real life—on which Ibsen drew for the composition of *Peer Gynt.* Nevertheless it is clear that by far the most important source for all those multifarious elements that go to make up the work was his own independent creative imagination. From legend, he actually took little more than the name of the chief character: that of a man who still reputedly lived on in peasant memory in Gudbrandsdal, and who Ibsen believed must still have been alive at the beginning of the century or thereabouts. ⟨. . .⟩

The world which Peer Gynt inhabits is one of daunting fluidity, a fairy-tale world of effortless transformations and of disconcerting transpositions; ⟨. . .⟩ Working and dreaming interpenetrate, fact and fantasy fuse, and all distinctions are blurred. The line between appearance and actuality, between fiction and fact, disappears in one great universe of the imagination. Fears are reborn as only nightmares can shape them; desires are achieved as only dream can fulfill them. The frustrations of one moment become the achievements of the next. If the girls at the village wedding spurn him, the girls on the mountain are ardent and willing. Ostracized and rejected as a suitor by the local community one day, he is welcomed as a potential son-in-law by the troll society the next. Disbelieved and mocked by the village youths when he brags of his exploits, he wins a flattering credulity from the Woman in Green, so that together they can agree that 'black can seem white, and the ugly beautiful; big can seem little, and filth seems clean'. As his mother Aase knows full well, Peer is intoxicated by make-believe as other man are drunk on brandy. His is a world in which wishes are horses (or, failing that, pigs!) and beggars *do* ride. Things, he discovers, are no sooner said than they *are* done—like the remotely triggered explosion which sinks the expropriated yacht. For him, distant lands are only a dream away. Fantasy worlds counterfeit the real world; the real one mints again the fantastic. Some creatures, such as the Dovre-Master and the Woman in Green, apparently live a valid life in both; in the case of others, appearances—but only appearances—change, whereby the village wedding guests become recognizable again in the trolls. Sometimes, as with the sound of church bells, reality penetrates fantasy; at other times, as with the Ugly Child, fantasy invades reality. All is an aspect of a single reality/fantasy continuum, wherein fact is a function of fiction, invention of experience, and lies and life are one.

—James McFarlane, "Introduction to *Peer Gynt*, by Henrik Ibsen." Translated by Christopher Fry and Johan Fillinger (Oxford: Oxford University Press, 1989): x–xii.

[Bjørn Hemmer has held the chairs of literature at the Universities of Trondheim and Oslo. He has written extensively on Ibsen, and is currently joint editor of the biennial *Contemporary Approaches to Ibsen*. In this excerpt, Hemmer discusses Ibsen's disillusionment with Scandinavianism.]

⟨In 1864⟩ the Norwegians failed to keep their promise to come to the aid of the Danes in their war against the Prussians. For Ibsen, this betokened not only a defeat for Scandinavianism; more specifically, it dealt a fatal blow to his faith in the power of nationalism and thereby to everything that had served him as the basis for his own literary activity. History had served as guarantor for the high ideals which he (along with many others) had cherished in respect of the people's potential, both present and future. Contemporary events were evidence that this was a delusion. Ibsen further concluded that this must also necessarily have consequences for literature. His letters of this time declare that the Norwegians must now strike out their past history, and writers must find a new foundation on which to base their work:

> *Back home* [i.e. in Norway] *I am afraid that from now on literature will have to take a new path;* there is at the present time no valid need or intrinsic necessity to go calling up the memory of our historic past; the things that have occurred there in the last two or three years—or, more correctly, those things that have not occurred— show pretty clearly that between the present generation of Norwegians and our mighty past, there is no closer connection than that between the Greek pirates of our day and the Ancients with their courage and faith and will, and with gods in their ranks. [my italics]

For Ibsen, national history thereby lost its monumental and didactic function. In the period immediately after leaving Norway, he was clearly uncertain which direction his writing should take. Many plans were considered, but there was no advance. In 1864, whilst still resident in Rome, he had renewed thoughts of seeking the subject matter for his work in past history. His encounter with Italy had lent actuality to Roman history, and he began to show an interest in Julian the Apostate, the revolutionary and dreamer; but for the time being this plan was put aside. First, Ibsen had to settle his account with contemporary Norway and its many blemishes. He was to write three more plays before returning, in the early 1870s, to the history of the Emperor who took up battle with the Galilean.

Brand (1866), *Peer Gynt* (1867) and *The League of Youth* (1869) all embody attacks on certain phenomena in contemporary Norway—and may well be interpreted as bitter criticism of the Norwegian national character. But what is also clear is that, whilst at work on these plays, Ibsen distanced himself from matters collectively nationalistic and became more occupied with people as individuals, with Kierkegaard's 'hin Enkelte'.

What he had recently seen happening in Norway was put into strong relief for him by recent events in Italy, where in the struggle for liberty and independence under Garibaldi's leadership the individual had shown a great sense of dedication and self-sacrifice. In a letter written in 1865, Ibsen wrote that there was something here which the Italians had taught him: that it was essential 'to possess a whole soul'. Thus national problems became more generalized and were relocated on an individual plane: it was on the individual that demands were properly made. Here Ibsen found what he himself called 'firm ground beneath one's feet'—and a new basis for his writing. Now it was no longer a question of a nation's renaissance but an *individual's* renaissance.

—Bjorn Hemmer, "Ibsen and Historical Drama." In *The Cambridge Companion to Ibsen*, ed. James McFarlane (Cambridge: Cambridge University Press, 1994): 21–23.

ERROLL DURBACH ON THE ENDING OF THE PLAY

[Erroll Durbach teaches in the Department of Theater at the University of British Columbia in Canada. In this excerpt, Durbach discusses the end of *Peer Gynt* and the possibilities of redemption.]

Near the end of his journey Peer passes a graveyard where a priest is speaking of the Soul's doom after its body's pilgrimage on earth. The occasion is the burial of a farmer who had once disgraced himself as a youth by an act of evasion, mutilating his hand to escape serving his country in war-time and so bearing his brand of shame for ever after. But in a life-time of reparation, dedicated to recreating value in the inconspicuous activities of daily living, this man has rediscovered meaning—not in troll-like self-sufficiency, but through quiet courage and determination. Neither flood nor avalanche can crack his soul. He cultivates the earth against fearful natural disaster. He educates his children with terrible physical difficulty, carrying them on his back to school through snowdrifts and ravines. Where Peer has evaded life's challenges and responsibilities this peasant farmer has confronted them and *changed the contents of his very being.* Selfhood is not fixed for all time by an act of cowardice but has been transformed by action within the small compass of his world:

> There he was great, because he was himself.
> His inborn note was steadfast as a star.
> (. . .)
> This man stands now no cripple to his God!

The dream of wholeness—Allmers's yearning hope for his own maimed child—becomes a living reality for this most unassuming of men who finds the capacity to change his condition by choosing the best self and embodying that choice in action. Kierkegaardian "Self-becoming," thrown into sharp relief by "being nothing," is one of those conceptual opposites that redeems the dread at the core of the onion.

Another saving value lies in the enigmatic theology of the Button-Moulder's response to Peer's overwhelming Modernist question:

> PEER GYNT: (pondering) What is it, "to be yourself," in truth?
> (. . .)
> BUTTON-MOULDER: To be yourself is to slay yourself.
>   But on you, that answer's sure to fail;
>   So let's say: to make your life evolve
>   From the Master's meaning to the last detail.
> PEER GYNT: But suppose a man never gets to know
>   What the Master meant with him?
> BUTTON-MOULDER: He must use intuition.

"Being oneself"—to paraphrase this notoriously difficult creed—means acknowledging existence as a process of continuous self-transformation, a recurrent annihilation of inauthentic and merely sufficient selfhoods, until selfishness itself is transcended. ⟨. . .⟩

The play is over, and Peer's life virtually done as he flees from the last meeting at the crossroads with the Button-moulder, a dead man long before he died. But just as he realizes that the backwards/forwards/roundabout routing of his life has led him nowhere, he encounters the woman he had run from at the start of the play—Solveig: all love, all compassion, the last living opportunity for discovering the Self in its vital relationship to others. In her presence, nowhere becomes somewhere, the form-less journey finds its map, and shattered selfhood becomes whole again in the consciousness of being loved. Peer's revelation, finally, connects the divided Selfhoods that in conjunction con-stitute the mythic wholeness from which modern man has fallen: the Existential "being in the world" that quests and searches after the Self's significance, and the Essential "being in the mind of God"—"været, som han sprang i Guds tanke frem"—that encodes the eternal value of Selfhood flowing through time. In Solveig, Peer encounters the repository of his enduring and continuous being, the lover's correlative to the Button-moulder's mystery:

PEER GYNT: Tell me where
Peer Gynt has been this many a year?
SOLVEIG: Been?
PEER GYNT: With his destiny on him, just
As when he first sprang from the mind of God
Can you tell me that?
(...)
Where have I been myself, whole and true?
Where have I been, with God's mark on my brow?
SOLVEIG: In my faith, in my hope, and in my love.

The connection of the lover's Self with the Self beloved, of the Soul with its human repository, is as ancient a resolution as it is modern —an echo, implicit in many of Ibsen's erotic dénouements, of a poetic love-tradition that places a nineteenth-century Norwegian dramatist in the company, not only of Lawrence, but of Petrarch and Donne.

—Erroll Durbach, "The Modernist Malaise: 'Nichts og Ingenting' at the Core of Ibsen's Onion." In *Contemporary Approaches to Ibsen*, vol. 9, eds. Bjorn Hemmer and Vigdis Ystad (Oslo: Scandinavian University Press, 1997): 10–12.

Works by
Henrik Ibsen

These are listed in the order they were published. The date of the first publication is listed first and the date of the first performance is second.

Catiline	1850/1881
The Feast of Solhaug	1856/1856
Lady Inger of Ostraat	1857/1855
The Vikings of Helgeland	1858/1858
Love's Comedy	1862/1873
The Pretenders	1863/1864
Brand	1866/1885
Peer Gynt	1867/1876
The League of Youth	1869/1869
Emperor and Galilean	1873/1896
Pillars of Society	1877/1877
A Doll House	1879/1879
Ghosts	1881/1882
An Enemy of the People	1882/1883
The Wild Duck	1884/1885
Rosmersholm	1886/1887
The Lady from the Sea	1888/1889
Hedda Gabler	1890/1891
The Master Builder	1892/1893
Little Eyolf	1894/1895
John Gabriel Borkman	1896/1897
When We Dead Awaken	1899/1900
Olaf Liljekrans	1902/1857
The Warrior's Barrow	1909/1850
St. John's Eve	1909/1853

Works about
Henrik Ibsen

Bentley, Eric. *The Playwright as Thinker*. New York: Reynal & Hitchcock, 1946.

———. *The Modern Theatre*. New Haven, CT: Yale University Press, 1948.

Bradbook, M.C. *Ibsen the Norwegian, A Revaluation*. New Edition. London: Chatto and Windus, 1966.

Brandes, Georg. *Henrik Ibsen: A Critical Study*. New York: Benjamin Blom, 1964 [1899].

Clurman, Harold. *Ibsen*. New York: The Macmillan Company, 1977.

Downs, Brian W. *Ibsen, The Intellectual Background*. New York: Cambridge University Press, 1948.

———. *A Study of Six Plays by Ibsen*. New York: Cambridge University Press, 1950.

Durbach, Erroll, ed. *Ibsen and the Theatre: The Dramatist in Production*. New York: New York University Press, 1980.

Egan, Michael, ed. *Ibsen, the Critical Heritage*. Boston: Routledge & Kegan Paul, 1972.

Fjelde, Rolf, ed. *Ibsen: A Collection of Critical Essays*. Englewood Cliffs, N.J.: Prentice-Hall, 1965.

———. "Peer Gynt, Naturalism and the Dissolving Self," in *The Drama Review*, XIII, 2 (Winter 1968): 28–43.

Hemmer, Bjorn, and Vigdis Ystad, eds. *Contemporary Approaches to Ibsen*, a biennial publication, Vols. I–IX. Oslo: Scandinavian University Press, 1966–1997.

Holtan, Orley. *Mythic Patterns in Ibsen's Last Plays*. Minneapolis: University of Minnesota Press, 1970.

Hurt, James. *Catiline's Dream, An Essay on Ibsen's Plays*. Urbana, IL: University of Illinois Press, 1972.

Ibsen, Bergliot. *The Three Ibsens, Memories of Henrik Ibsen, Suzannah Ibsen and Sigurd Ibsen.* Trans. Gerik Schjelderup. New York: American-Scandinavian Foundation, 1952.

James, Henry. *The Scenic Art.* New York: Hill and Wang, 1948.

Johnston, Brian. *The Ibsen Cycle: The Design of the Plays from* Pillars of Society *to* When We Dead Awaken. Boston: Twayne/G.K. Hall & Co., 1975.

———. *To the Third Empire.* Minneapolis: University of Minnesota, 1980.

Jorgenson, Theodore. *Henrik Ibsen: A Study in Art and Personality.* Northfield, MN: St. Olaf College Press, 1945.

Joyce, James. "Ibsen's New Drama." *Fortnightly Review* 67 (April 1, 1900): 575–590.

Knight, G. Wilson. *Henrik Ibsen.* Edinburgh: Oliver & Boyd, 1962.

Koht, Halvdan. *Life of Ibsen.* Trans. and ed. Einar Haugen and A. E. Santiello. New York: Benjamin Blom, 1971.

Lucas, F. W. *The Drama of Ibsen and Strindberg.* New York: The Macmillan Company; London: Cassell and Company, 1962.

Lyons, Charles R. *Henrik Ibsen, The Divided Consciousness.* Carbondale, IL: Southern Illinois University Press, 1972.

McFarlane, James W. ed. *Henrik Ibsen, A Critical Anthology.* Harmondsworth, Middlesex: Penguin Books, 1970.

———. *Ibsen and the Temper of Norwegian Literature.* New York: Oxford University Press, 1960.

———, ed. *The Cambridge Companion to Ibsen.* Cambridge: Cambridge University Press, 1994.

Meyer, Michael. *Ibsen: A Biography.* Garden City, N.Y.: Hill and Wang, 1964.

Northam, John. *Ibsen's Dramatic Method.* London: Faber and Faber, 1953.

Shaw, George Bernard. *The Quintessence of Ibsenism.* New York: Hill and Wang, 1957 (1913).

Tennant, P. F. D. *Ibsen's Dramatic Technique*. Cambridge: Bowes and Bowes, 1948.

Valency, Maurice. *The Flower and the Castle, An Introduction to the Modern Drama: Ibsen and Strindberg*. New York: Macmillan Company, 1963.

Van Laan, Thomas F. "The Death of Tragedy Myth," in *Journal of Dramatic Theory and Criticism* 4, no. 2 (1991): 5–31.

Ystad, Vigdis, ed. *Ibsen, at the Centre for Advanced Study*. Oslo: Scandinavian University Press, 1997.

Zucker, Adolf E. *Ibsen the Master Builder*. New York: Octagon Books, 1973 (1929).

Index of
Themes and Ideas

56, 58, 60, 76; Kaja Fosli in, 30, 32, 35, 40; Dr. Herdal in, 30, 33, 35, 40, 41, 49; past events in, 48–49; plot summary of, 30–34; poetic style of, 76; Aline Solness in, 30, 31, 33, 34, 35, 36, 39, 44, 46, 48, 76; Halvard Solness in, 9, 23, 30–34, 35, 36–37, 39, 40–41, 45–47, 48, 49, 56, 58, 60; Halvard Solness's lust for youth in, 45–47; troll in, 31; Hilda Wangel in, 30–34, 35, 37, 38–39, 40–41, 45, 46, 47, 48–49, 76

PEER GYNT, 63–82; Aase in, 63, 70, 72, 78; Mr. Ballon in, 64, 70; Professor Begriffenfeldt in, 64, 68, 70; bird cries in, 70; Button Molder in, 64–65, 68, 71, 73, 75, 82, 86; characters in, 70–71; Mr. Cotton in, 64, 70; critical views on, 9, 23, 44, 57–58, 72–82; Herr von Eberkopf in, 64, 70; ending of, 80–82; farm boy in, 67, 71, 80–81; farmer in, 70; Fellah in, 71; fence in, 64, 70; Great Boyg in, 64, 66, 67, 70; Peer Gynt as tragic hero in, 74–75; Peer Gynt in, 9, 22, 23, 44, 57–58, 63–69, 70, 72–75, 78, 81–82; Peer Gynt's inability to change in, 72–73; Helga in, 70; Huhu in, 71; Hussein in, 71; Ingrid in, 66, 70; inmates in, 64, 68, 71; Kari in, 70; keepers in, 64, 71; lean person in, 71; newcomer and wife in, 70; Norwegian sea captain in, 71; Pastor in, 67, 72–73, 80–81; plot summary of, 63–69; poetic style of, 75–76; psychology of, 72–73; Solveig in, 63, 64, 65, 68–69, 70, 73, 75, 82; sources for, 77–78; Sphinx at Gizeh in, 64, 68, 70; statue of memnon in, 70; strange passenger in, 71; thief in, 64, 70; three herd girls in, 70, 78; troll in, 66–67, 78; Troll King in, 63, 67, 68, 70; Herr Trumpeterstraale in, 64, 70; Voice in the Darkness in, 63–64, 66, 67, 70; wedding guests in, 63, 66, 70, 79; Woman in Green in, 63, 70, 78

PILLARS OF SOCIETY, 12, 22, 55

ROSMERSHOLM, 23, 76

WARRIOR'S BARROW, THE, 11

WHEN WE DEAD AWAKEN, 50–61; characters in, 53; critical views on, 9, 46, 54–61; Irene in, 50, 51–52, 53, 59, 60; manager in, 53; nun in, 53; plot summary of, 50–52; Major Rubek in, 50, 51, 52, 53; Professor Arnold Rubek in, 9, 23, 50–51, 52, 53, 56, 58, 59–61; Professor Arnold Rubek's vision in, 59–61; Ulfhejm in, 50, 51–52, 53